On the night before he died, Jesus Christ shared with his disciples—and with us—the fantastic secret that enables ordinary men to fulfill the rigorous demands of the Christian life.

In SECRETS OF THE SPIRIT, Ray Stedman penetrates passages of Scripture and comes up with a meaningful interpretation to aid modern-day disciples in understanding more clearly Christ's plan for our future, his total understanding of our needs, his preparation and provision for us, and how to carry on his Word and work on earth.

The final words of Jesus Christ, as amplified and explained in SECRETS OF THE SPIRIT, present answers not only to the wide-sweeping problems of mankind, but also to the personal needs and concerns felt by everyone of us.

About the Author:

Ray C. Stedman emphasizes a strong laymen's training program in his capacity as pastor of Peninsula Bible Church in Palo Alto, California. A graduate of Dallas Theological Seminary and recipient of a Doctor of Divinity degree from Talbot Theological Seminary, he has traveled throughout the Orient, Europe and Latin America, holding pastor's conferences and witnessing. He is the author of several well-received books, including AUTHENTIC CHRISTIANITY.

SECRETS OF THE SPIRIT

Ray C. Stedman

A KEY-WORD BOOK
WORD BOOKS, publisher
Waco, Texas

SECRETS OF THE SPIRIT

A KEY-WORD BOOK

Published by Pillar Books for Word Books, Publishers by arrangement with Fleming H. Revell.

Copyright © 1975 by Ray C. Stedman

First Key-Word Book edition, May 1977

Library of Congress Catalog Card Number: 74-20925

ISBN: 0-87680-803-8

Printed in the United States of America

Contents

Preface

The passage known as the Upper Room Discourse in the Gospel of John, chapters 13 through 17, takes us into the intimate thoughts of Jesus just before his Crucifixion. Some have called this the "holy of holies" of Scripture. That is, if you think of Scripture as a temple, this is the sanctuary, where you come into the very presence of God himself. By means of his words to his disciples, we are permitted here to enter into the thinking and emotions of Jesus just before his own Crucifixion. Within hours of this event, the Lord was hanging upon a cross. In less than twenty-four hours he was dead and buried. These therefore constitute the last words of Jesus before his own death.

Because all power in heaven and earth had been placed in the hands of Jesus, he was, in a sense, directing his own death. He was in charge of the events. Rather than being a helpless victim of circumstances over which he had no control, he was himself determining them as they went along. Remember how, in the Garden, when the soldiers came to get him, Jesus spoke to them with such authority that they all fell backward upon the ground! Who was in charge there? Then he gave orders to the soldiers to dismiss the rest of the apostles and let them go, and the soldiers obeyed. He was in command throughout all this amazing series of events.

In this deep and penetrating passage, our Lord is laying his heart bare before his disciples. He is seeking to impart to them the secret of his life—the secret which is the explanation of those amazing words that he spoke and those amazing works which he did. That secret lies in his relationship to his Father. And that relationship is what Jesus stresses as he talks with these disciples.

In this passage some tremendous concepts are brought out for their understanding, and for ours as well. He

7

tells them that a replacement for himself is coming to them—the Holy Spirit. Another Comforter, another Strengthener is on the way. And when he comes he will no longer be merely *with* them but *within* them. Their strength will no longer come from without, as when Jesus was their Comforter, but will come from within.

Thus he marks the prominent characteristic of the Day of the Spirit, in which we live. He tells them that **the primary work of the Spirit will be to take the life of Jesus and release it to these believers.** This is the great and marvelous truth which the Scriptures seek to set before us. When the Spirit came to release Jesus' life within his disciples, they were then able to live by him, as he lived by means of the Father. This is the fantastic secret which makes possible the fulfillment of the high demands of Christian living. A Christian lives by the same principle as Jesus did. As he lived by means of the Father, in dependence and trust in him, moment by moment, so we are to live by means of the Son, in dependence and trust in him.

As we look carefully, then, at this passage—a few verses at a time—we will begin to see more clearly into the heart of our Lord, into his total understanding of our needs; to see his preparations and provision for us, and to understand more clearly how we are to bear the fruit which remains.

1

The Towel Wearer
John 13:1–20

The passage in John's Gospel often referred to as the Upper Room Discourse actually begins with a parable in action. Rather than a discourse or a message, it begins with the deeds of Jesus, the act of Jesus washing the disciples' feet. In that remarkable event, simple as it was—and yet strange in many ways—the Apostle John sees very deep and remarkable meaning.

There are two movements in this event, which John gathers up in the preface to this account. First he sees the evidence and the demonstration of the unchanging love of Jesus for his disciples. Second, he sees a revelation of reality, especially as it related to Judas. Of the first, he says:

> *Now before the feast of the Passover, when Jesus knew that his hour had come to depart out of this world to the Father, having loved his own who were in the world, he loved them to the end.*
> *John 13:1*

Don't be confused, as some have been, by the opening words: *before the feast of the Passover*. Some have struggled with the chronology of this event, feeling that these words date the feast of the Lord's Supper as having taken place before the feast of the Passover, which would be contrary to what the other Gospels record.

But John is not linking this phrase with the subsequent event of the Lord's Supper and the washing of the disciples' feet. He is referring back to the time when Jesus discovered that his hour had come. That information is recorded in chaper 12—when the Greeks came and asked to see Jesus. When Philip and Andrew told Jesus that certain Gentiles were asking for him, this was for him the signal for the beginning of the dramatic denouement of his ministry, the sign that it was now drawing rapidly to an end. He answered them: *The hour has come for the Son of man to be glorified* (John 12:23).

All John is saying here is that from that moment on, Jesus understands that the time has come, the hour has struck, that he is now to make his exodus from the world by means of death and resurrection. He has always known what the events would be, but he has not known the time they would come. Now he knows.

From that moment on, he nevertheless remains considerate and compassionate toward his own disciples. That strikes John dramatically. He is amazed by the fact that Jesus is not thinking of himself, though he knows that this is the hour toward which his whole life has been pointing. Rather, his thoughts are still upon his disciples. He teaches them and manifests love, compassion, and concern for them to the very end. That is the first thing which John sees in this remarkable scene of the washing of the disciples' feet. Jesus is still loving his disciples. Now the Passover has come, and Jesus is meeting with his disciples to eat the Passover meal together:

> *And during supper, when the devil had already put it into the heart of Judas Iscariot, Simon's son, to betray him, Jesus, knowing that the Father had given all things into his hands, and that he had come from God and was going to God, rose from supper, laid aside his garments, and girded himself with a towel.*   John 13:2-4

The second movement concerns Judas. John sees in the act of foot washing a demonstration of the truth which is in Jesus, of the remarkable passion which strips away all pretense and hypocrisy and reveals things exactly the way they are.

In this dramatic act of washing his disciples' feet— Judas included—John sees a manifestation of the love of Jesus that seeks yet to reach the traitor, and the

truth of God, the honesty of God which exposes hypocrisy. By means of such action Jesus seeks to lay hold
of Judas's heart and show him what is happening to
him. Jesus is moved to do this, John says, by the
awareness of his authority. All things were given into
his hands by the Father; he knows that. He knows
who he is, knows he has come from God, knows he is
going to God. Moved, then, by this sense of his own
identity and authority, he begins to expose (by direct
words to him) what Judas is doing and where he is
headed at the same time that he teaches the other
apostles how to care for one another. John sees all this
as intertwined together in this remarkable scene: the
commitment of love which teaches to the end, and the
passion of truth which fights to the end for the deliverance of Judas.

The Parable Worked Out

Following this preface is the account of the foot
washing itself. Jesus rose from supper, laid aside his
garments, and girded himself with a towel.

*Then he poured water into a basin, and began to
wash the disciples' feet, and to wipe them with
the towel with which he was girded.* John 13:5

There can be little doubt that here Jesus was deliberately working out a parable for the instruction of
his disciples. He was dramatizing for them the character of his ministry. He was showing them by this
means what he had come into the world to do, and
what he would send them out to do.

We can trace the parable in the events which John
records. First, Jesus *rose from supper,* just as he had
once risen from his throne of glory. Then he *laid aside
his garments.* Paul tells us that when he came into
the world in the incarnate state he laid aside the
exercise of his deity. He did not come to act as God;
he came to live as man, indwelt by God. Then he
girded himself with a towel, just as Paul later records
that: *taking the form of a servant...he humbled
himself and became obedient unto death* (Philippians

2:7, 8). So here he humbles himself, taking the role
of a slave and girding himself with a towel.

Then he poured water into a basin, as in a few
hours he was to pour out his blood in death, the blood
which would be for the cleansing of human defilement,
of human guilt of every kind and source. Next he
*began to wash the disciples' feet, and to wipe them
with the towel with which he was girded,* picturing
the act of applying the cleansing of his blood to human
hearts. If we skip to verse 12 we see the end of the
parable. *When he had washed their feet, and taken his
garments,* he *resumed his place,* just as the writer of
Hebrews records for us: *When he had made purifica-
tion for sins, he sat down at the right hand of the
Majesty on high* (Hebrews 1:3). Thus we have this
remarkable, beautiful parable worked out for us,
teaching us the meaning of his whole ministry.

Not me, Lord!

In the act of foot washing, Peter was brought into
the picture. Moving around the circle of disciples, the
Lord came at last to Peter, who promptly refused to
let him wash his feet:

> . . . *Peter said to him, "Lord, do you wash my
> feet?" Jesus answered him, "What I am doing
> you do not know now, but afterward you will
> understand." Peter said to him, "You shall never
> wash my feet." Jesus answered him, "If I do not
> wash you, you have no part [with] me."*
>   John 13:6-8

(I know that the Revised Standard Version uses the
phrase *in me,* but the Greek text clearly and unmis-
takably says *with.* This is a very important distinction, as we shall see in a moment.)

Peter's refusal to be washed by Jesus pictures both
the need of Christians for the cleansing which Jesus
offers, and the sinful pride which often rejects that
cleansing. Peter's actions were prompted ostensibly by
humility. At first glance, it appears as though Peter's
expostulation arose out of his sense of inadequacy and

unworthiness before Jesus. You can see the incredulity on his face when Jesus approached him, and he protested, "Lord, you'll never do this to me!" This sounds like a humble statement, reflecting Peter's feeling that Jesus ought never to take such a low position as to wash his feet. But when you look a bit closer, you can see that it is really an expression of intense personal pride. Peter is offended by Jesus' actions, because he knows that if he were in the same place, if he were an instructor, a teacher, a Lord, he would never consider stooping to wash someone's feet. It would be beneath him. Jesus has violated Peter's image of a leader and he feels uncomfortable and unhappy. He doesn't want Jesus to wash his feet. He would be quite content to wash Jesus' feet, but it is an affront to his conception of authority that Jesus should ever do anything for him—just as, later on, Peter offers to lay down his life for Jesus; he doesn't want Jesus to lay down his life for him.

What a revelation this is of the pride of our hearts which cloaks itself in a guise of humility when we are really insisting upon our self-sufficiency. We do not want to admit to anyone that we are in need of anything. Peter does not want to let Jesus do this menial act for him. It humiliates him. So he stands as a clear example of the pride in our hearts which resists the ministry of Jesus to us.

We Need to Be Humiliated

One of the remarkable things about the Gospel is that it always brings us to the lowest point. We must stand before God in utter humiliation and abjectness in order for him to minister to us. All human pride must be brought low before we can receive what God wants to give us from his hand. But that is where we struggle. We don't like that. We don't like to be brought to a place where we have nothing to offer. We always want to add something of our own. Peter is a clear picture of this.

When Jesus explains to him: *if I do not wash you, you can have no part* [with] *me*, Peter immediately capitulates, and flops to the other extreme. He cannot bear the thought that he will have no part with Jesus.

*Simon Peter said to him, "Lord, not my feet only
but also my hands and my head!"*   John 13:9

In other words, he asks for a bath. Jesus had said
earlier: *What I do now you don't understand,* and
Peter proves indeed that he doesn't understand what
is happening. So Jesus corrects him again:

*Jesus said to him, "He who has bathed does not
need to wash, except for his feet, but he is clean
all over. . . ."*   John 13:10

In those words Jesus gives us a beautiful explanation
of the process of salvation. It begins with a bath. That
initial coming to Christ (in which we take the place
of bankruptcy before him, coming without a vestige of
our righteousness to offer, but allowing him to cleanse
us) is likened to a bath in which we are washed all
over completely, from head to foot.

Jesus is alluding to a very common social practice in
those days. It was the custom to take a bath before
you went out to a meal. But in walking through the
dirty streets of the city with sandals on, your feet
would be defiled. And so when you arrived as a guest,
a servant would wash your feet. But you would *not*
need to repeat the bath. Jesus is thus saying, "When
you first come to me and believe, you are bathed, you are
cleansed all over." This is what the Bible calls justification by faith. It is a washing away of all guilt, all
defilement, and all the sin of an entire life—past,
present, and future. But as you walk on through life,
Jesus knows there will be defilement incurred in the
walk which also needs to be washed away. The bath
gives us part *in* him, the foot washing gives us part
with him.

Our Part With Him

In this way he teaches us that not only do we need
that initial never-to-be-repeated cleansing which washes
us as a bath; but we need also the many-times-re-
peated experience of forgiveness, of coming to Christ
for the cleansing away of the defilement of our walk.
It is this which determines that we have part *with* him.

The enjoyment of our relationship with Christ is lost when we are temporarily defiled by wrongdoing and by attitudes which are wrong in our life. We lose the enjoyment of our relationship with him. That is part *with* him. His attitude toward us doesn't change, but our attitude toward him does. That is why we are taught in the Scriptures: *If we confess our sins, he is faithful and just, and will forgive our sins and cleanse us from all unrighteousness* (1 John 1:9). And the moment we do so we are renewed; that is, the original cleansing is renewed to us, and we feel once again the renewing of our spirits, the lifting up of the vitality of our spiritual lives, and we go on again, restored.

Peter's error is still being repeated today. There are those who, like him, refuse to allow Jesus to wash their feet. They are rejecting the indispensable requisite for enjoying their relationship with Christ. When people refuse to let Jesus wash their feet, they lose that sense of partnership with him.

The Holy Spirit Did Not Stutter

On the other hand, there are those who, like Peter, feel that they need a bath all over again when they sin, that they have lost their salvation and that somehow they have to start all over in their Christian experience. Every now and then I run into people who are laboring under that delusion, who think that they need to be born, not only again, but again and again and again, as though the Holy Spirit had stuttered when he said, "regeneration," and had said, "re-re-re-re-regeneration"! But Jesus teaches us by this whole process that only one bath is needed. This is reflected in the truth of baptism. We are baptized once, as the initial act. But the Lord's Supper reflects the washing of the feet, and the need for the cleansing again and again through life from the defilement and the guilt of sin.

In the closing portion of this section our Lord explains what he has done:

When he had washed their feet, and taken his garments, and resumed his place, he said to them, "Do you know what I have done to you?

You call me Teacher and Lord; and you are right, for so I am. If I then, your Lord and Teacher, have washed your feet, you also ought to wash one another's feet. For I have given you an example, that you also should do as I have done to you. Truly, truly, I say to you, a servant is not greater than his master; nor is he who is sent greater than he who sent him. If you know these things, blessed are you if you do them."

                                          John 13:12-17

In this explanation Jesus begins again with his own authority. "You call me Teacher and Lord; and you are right. I *am* your Teacher, I *am* your Lord—your Teacher, with the right to instruct you; your Lord, with the right to command you." He acknowledges his identity before them and asserts that he has this right in their lives. But his argument is, "If I, then, with this acknowledged position of authority in your lives, have washed your feet, then you also are to wash one another's feet."

A New Sacrament?

Now, what does he mean when he says that we ought to wash one another's feet? Some Christians have taken this very literally and have thought that our Lord was instituting another sacrament here, along with baptism and the Lord's Supper. You will occasionally find groups of Christians who, very sincerely, have what they call foot-washing services, where they wash one another's feet. I once attended one of these services, and I noted that those who came were very careful to wash their own feet beforehand. They would never have thought of coming with dirty feet to a foot-washing service! But Jesus washed the dirty feet of his disciples, without any opportunity for preparation on their part. He took the role of a servant to that degree.

No, Jesus is not giving us another sacrament to follow here, not another mere ceremony which would be meaningless because it wouldn't reflect what was originally in view. What he means is that just as we need cleansing and forgiveness from our Lord in order to maintain the sense of unity and refreshment of spirit in our Christian life, so we need to extend to one another free forgiveness for guilt and for the injury that we may do to one another. We are to be, in the words of Paul, *tenderhearted, forgiving one another, even as God in Christ forgave you* (Ephesians 4:32). Isn't this what Jesus teaches us in the Lord's Prayer? *Forgive us our trespasses, even as we forgive those who have trespassed against us* (*see* Matthew 6:12). He is exhorting Christians to forgive each other, and their authority to do so is based upon his own example.

He knows that it is difficult sometimes to forgive—that the flesh within cries out for revenge. We want people to pay for what they have done to us. We want to extract some kind of return for the injury. We love the feeling of carrying a grudge, or of resisting the overtures of the other person. We like the feeling of telling them off, giving them a piece of our mind, ripping into them.

But Jesus says that when we do that, we are doing what he would never do. We are asserting our prerogatives, we are demanding our rights, we are insisting upon the privilege and status that we feel we should have. We are forgetting that though our Lord and Master was rightfully our Teacher and our Lord, rightfully the Lord of Glory, the One with every claim on the worship of men, nevertheless he laid it all aside —did not demand it, did not seek it, did not insist upon it—and washed the feet of his disciples. So he says that we must do the same for one another.

No Christian has a right to sit in self-righteous judgment upon others. We may bring them, and we are exhorted to do so, under the searching light of the Word of God. We may, out of concern and compassion for their welfare, expose to them what they are doing, as Jesus does here with his disciples. But in no sense are we to do so in self-righteousness, with the suggestion that *we* could never do such a thing. Nor are we to demand that they first apologize before we forgive, or that in some way they repay us, or straighten out what they have done, before we extend to them free and open acceptance and forgiveness.

So when we resist this kind of ministry (we don't

want to forgive or we don't want somebody to come and wash our feet with the Word) we are doing what Peter did, refusing to follow the admonition of our Lord. We make ourselves greater than our Master, ignoring his word here:

> *Truly, truly, I say to you, a servant is not greater than his master; nor is he who is sent greater than he who sent him. If you know these things, blessed are you if you do them.*   John 13:16, 17

Dr. H. A. Ironside has pointed out how wise it is, when washing another's feet, to exercise concern as to the temperature of the water! Some go with boiling hot water. They are angry and so upset by what has happened that they come and say, "Here, stick your feet in here!" Nobody wants to have his feet washed with boiling water. Some go to the other extreme and come with ice water. They are so righteously holier-than-thou, so remote from the whole dirty proposition, so above it all! No one wants to respond to that either.

And some, unfortunately, try to do it without any water at all! They come and dry-clean your feet; they *scrape* them free of dirt. Have you ever had anyone do that to you? They come and give you a piece of their mind and just tear into you. What they say may be true, but there is no water of love to wash the dirt gently away, there is only a rigid insistence upon scraping it away and the skin along with it. But our Lord insists that we wash one another's feet in love. That is the way that he loved his disciples, and he loved them to the end.

Harmony in the Family

Notice the promised results: *If you know these things, blessed are you if you do them.* That is the secret of maintaining harmony among Christians, in a Christian family, and in the larger family of the church. We must actually act in this loving and responsible way toward one another. A young man once came to me from another church. He had been greatly distressed to find that one of the outstanding young laymen of his church, who had been appointed as a

sponsor of the youth group of that church, was guilty
of immorality with a young girl. This was threatening
his marriage, and rumors of it had spread among the
young people, so that the whole church was beginning
to stir.

It looked like a terrible disaster, a tragic occurrence
that would split the church apart when it all came to
light. This troubled young man asked me, "What
should I do?" I said, "Well, you've been given guide-
lines in the Scriptures as to what to do: *If your
brother sins against you, go and tell him his fault,
between you and him alone. If he listens to you, you
have gained your brother.* (*See* Matthew 18:15.) *That*
is washing his feet."

So he went back, and in a few weeks I got a letter
from him. He said, "I took your advice, I went to him
and simply told him what I knew. And I told him in
love. I didn't try to destroy him or condemn him. I
understood the pressures, the passions which moved
him to this wrongdoing, and I loved him. But I told
him what was happening in the congregation, and that
what he had done was wrong. He acknowledged it, and
together we went to the leaders of the church and laid
the whole matter before them. The result has been
that this man has voluntarily left his ministry for a
while until all this is straightened out in his life. But
he himself has been healed, and his marriage has been
saved and restored. The church has been strengthened
by all this, rather than split." That is what Jesus
means when he says: *If you know these things, blessed
are you if you do them.*

Jesus and Judas

The last part of the paragraph presents the contrast
provided by Judas. Jesus says:

*I am not speaking of you all; I know whom I
have chosen; it is that the scripture may be fulfilled, "He who ate my bread has lifted his heel
against me." I tell you this now, before it takes
place, that when it does take place you may believe that I am he. Truly, truly, I say to you, he*

who receives any one whom I send receives me;
and he who receives me receives him who sent me.
                                                    John 13:18-20

The contrast here is between the knowledge of Jesus
and the ignorant unbelief of Judas. Jesus knows what
is happening. He walks in the light of the Scriptures
and thus knows that one among those close to him will
betray him, and he knows from the beginning which
one it will be. But Judas doesn't know that. Judas is
ignorantly following the avarice and greed of his
heart, and resisting every effort Jesus makes to reach
him. Now he is on the verge of that final act of rejection which will plunge him over the precipice into
utter and complete disaster. Soon Judas will take the
morsel from Jesus' hand—and that is his final chance.
When he does that, Satan enters into him, and Judas is
no longer his own master in any degree at all. Jesus
here indicates that he understands what will happen.
He says, "I'm telling you this before it happens, so
that when it does, you will know I am the One this
Scripture describes, that I am the One the psalm is
speaking about." (*See* Psalms 41:9.) Judas is utterly
deaf to the warnings. He doesn't know what is happening to him, that he has fallen into Satan's snare and
now is at the very brink of disaster.

As you read this account, you can see how these
two stand opposed one to another. Jesus sacrifices himself in order to save his disciples; Judas sacrifices
Jesus in order to save himself. These two philosophies
dominate the world today.

In this final appeal, Jesus is directing a word to these
representative attitudes: *Truly, truly, I say to you, he*
who receives any one whom I send, receives me. That is
a word to the eleven disciples (and to us) that when
someone comes to us to wash our feet, to help us with
some problem of sin or error in our lives, we are to remember that this person is sent by Jesus. Therefore it
is Jesus himself who is standing before us. It is he who
is offering to wash our feet. We are not to resent this
ministry on the part of others. We are not to say, "You
have no right to come to me. This is my own private
affair; you have nothing to do with it." But we are to

remember that, *he who receives any one whom I send,*
[Jesus says] *receives me.* Let us not, like Peter, fall into
the error of rejecting the indispensable ministry of
cleansing which Jesus offers.

The last word is addressed to Judas: *And he who
receives me receives him who sent me.* That is, he receives God the Father himself. There is no other way
to the Father but by Jesus. This is the truth Jesus
declares again and again, and it is the great truth
which Judas seeks to circumvent. He tries to relate to
God without accepting Jesus. He tries to live his life
before God without relating to the ministry and salvation offered by Jesus.

There are many like that today, who, like Judas, are
stumbling blindly on, not realizing that they are facing the most important crisis of their lives, and that
only Jesus can bring them to God. Jesus says so himself: *I am the way, and the truth, and the life; no one
comes to the Father, but by me* (John 14:6). This
word about receiving him is Jesus' last-ditch stand to
reach Judas before it is too late. Though he fails, as
subsequent events will show, the great truth he leaves
before us is this: there is no other way to the Father,
but by him.

None other Lamb, none other Name.
None other Hope in heaven or earth or sea,
None other Hiding-place from guilt and shame,
None beside Thee.

                                        CHRISTINA ROSSETTI

Our Father, there may be some among us who have mingled with the people of God, have sought to live as they do but have never yet come into a saving relationship with the Lord Jesus. Thus they have refused the bath of forgiveness, of justification: have refused to acknowledge their need of cleansing, and have tried to cleanse themselves, to make their own lives right before you. Lord Jesus, we pray that you will deal with them just as you dealt with Judas, and will help them to see what they are doing. For those of us, Lord, who have come through the bath but who still need the ministry of others to us, help us to understand that it is you, Lord, who stands before us in our brother or sister who comes to admonish us, to exhort us, to seek to correct us and to lead us back into paths of righteousness and peace. May we not reject this ministry, Lord, for in so doing we reject you, as Peter did, and therefore have no sense of enjoyment in our lives. Heal our lives by this means we pray, Lord Jesus, in your name and for your sake. Amen.

2

Judas and Peter
John 13:21-38

In the first half of chapter 13, Jesus made clear to his disciples, as he stooped to wash their feet, that their relationship to one another was to be based on loving forgiveness. Although Jesus had the authority to lord it over them, he laid royalty aside to take the place of their servant, and he said: *I have given you an example, that you also should do as I have done to you* (John 13:15).

Now, in the closing part of this chapter, we can see, in three distinct movements, the depth of understanding Jesus had of the people and events and motivations surrounding his death. First we see that Jesus knew and understood the hostility of Judas, which would lead to the death of both men—one by suicide and one by crucifixion. Then, he knew the weakness of Peter. He understood what Peter had within him, and that this would lead to his threefold denial and his cursing.

In between these two insights we have a great but brief section in which it is evident that our Lord knew the principle of glory (the means by which true glory is achieved)—the principle which Judas rejected; and he understood the power of love, a principle of which Peter was ignorant. This power of love would be the radical secret that he would let loose upon the world. Let us take first the incident of Judas and Jesus together:

When Jesus had thus spoken, he was troubled in spirit, and testified, "Truly, truly, I say to you, one of you will betray me." The disciples looked at one another, uncertain of whom he spoke. One of his disciples, whom Jesus loved, was lying close to the breast of Jesus; so Simon Peter bec-

koned to him and said, "Tell us whom it is of
whom he speaks." So lying thus, close to the
breast of Jesus, he said to him, "Lord, who is it?"
Jesus answered, "It is he to whom I shall give
this morsel". . . . he gave it to Judas, the son of
Simon Iscariot.   John 13:21-26

John sets this account against the background of the
distress of Jesus. He records that when Jesus had finished the foot washing, and had sought to warn Judas,
he was *troubled in spirit*. The Greek word means that
he was deeply agitated, grieved, hurt. Going to the
cross was not an easy thing for Jesus to do. If we
think of him as being unmoved through this whole
circumstance, of speaking always with poise and an
untroubled spirit, we are wrong, for Jesus was deeply
disturbed at this point. It grieved him to face the
perfidy and treachery of Judas. He had just quoted
(from the Forty-First Psalm) the verse in which
David had said: *He who ate my bread has lifted his*
heel against me. In the mind of Jesus this was what
Judas was about to do. The phrase, "he has lifted his
heel against me" is a word-picture of a companion
who, without warning, for no reason, suddenly turns
around, lifts his heel, and kicks one in the face. You
can imagine what a stunning shock that would be.
Thus Jesus was greatly troubled as he anticipated this
action of Judas. He felt it with full force as an act
of callous betrayal by one whom he had loved and
trusted.

A Fading Dream for Judas

Jesus knew that the story of Judas was one of increasing greed. If you put together the many little
references to Judas in the Scriptures you can see what
was happening to this man. When he first joined the
Twelve he evidently was a sincere, dedicated follower.
He had a good business head and a reputation for
honesty. Therefore he was chosen to be the treasurer
of the Twelve and was given charge of the money box.
This indicated that the other disciples had confidence
in him. You never elect a treasurer who doesn't show
some indication of being able to handle money prop-

erly. (I have always been surprised and disturbed that I have never been elected treasurer of anything!) But Judas was elected treasurer of the apostolic band.

When he first joined the group, Judas evidently had seen in Jesus the chance to fulfill his dream. Judas believed that Jesus was the coming Messiah who would deliver Israel from its bondage and make it the head of the nations of the earth. He believed that world government would flow from Jerusalem. There were many great passages of the Old Testament which spoke of this. Judas, like other Jews, had read these wonderful passages of glory but had ignored those which dealt with the suffering Messiah. So he joined the band with the anticipation that he would be in the inner circle.

But then Jesus began to speak about the cross, and when Judas saw him offending the leaders of the Jews, and saw the growing opposition of the Pharisees toward Jesus, Judas knew that his dream was fading. He became inwardly resentful and bitter against Jesus. Finally he took matters into his own hands. John told us in the previous chapter that Judas had begun to steal money out of the money box. In the story of Mary, who wiped Jesus' feet with the ointment, we read:

> *But Judas Iscariot, one of his disciples (he who was to betray him), said, "Why was this ointment not sold for three hundred denarii and given to the poor?" This he said, not that he cared for the poor but because he was a thief, and as he had the money box he used to take what was put into it.*   John 12:4-6

So for some time Judas had been stealing out of the treasury. What for? Well, as we put the story together it is evident that he had contracted to buy a piece of property, evidently a parcel near Jerusalem in a fine location, which he thought would be a good spot to build on when the kingdom came. He had purchased it for himself. He was, in other words, feathering his own nest, utilizing the opportunity as treasurer of the band to take the money for this purpose.

As the Jews' hatred of Jesus grew, and Judas saw

that an inevitable climax must ensue, he grew impatient. Lacking thirty pieces of silver to complete his purchase, he went to the high priest and made a deal with him to betray Jesus for the money needed to purchase the property. Later, when the money was brought back by Judas and flung at their feet, the priests took it and went out and finished the payment, bought the property, and called it the Field of Blood, because it was there that Judas hanged himself. (*See* Matthew 27:3-10 and Acts 1:18, 19.)

The Place of Honor for Judas

Jesus knew that it was covetousness, avarice, greed, and hunger for worldly success that were motivating Judas. And yet Jesus was grieved and hurt, because he knew that the callous selfishness of Judas had come about only by his repeated rejection of Jesus' love. You can't read the story of these two men without seeing how persistent Jesus was in trying to reach Judas. Even there at the Last Supper it was apparent.

One sign of it was in the table arrangements which John records. Most people are familiar with Leonardo da Vinci's painting *The Last Supper*, and they think that is the way it actually occurred—all of them sitting on one side of a long table. It is almost certain that this is not the way it was, because the custom of the Jews was not to sit at a table, but to eat while half-reclining on couches around the table, in the way the Romans did. The table was very likely U-shaped. At the center of the closed end sat Jesus as the host, half-reclining on his left side on his couch, so that his right hand would be free to eat with. On the adjoining couch to the right was the Apostle John. He always refers to himself as *that disciple whom Jesus loved*. As he tells us here, he was sitting close to the breast of Jesus. His head would have been right at Jesus' chest level because of the arrangement of the couches. And on the other side, the left side of Jesus, which, incidentally, was the place of honor, was Judas. Jesus' head would have been at Judas' breast, as John's head was at the breast of Jesus. This arrangement made it possible for these three to carry on an intimate conversation, unheard by the others. Only that table arrangement explains what happened here at the Last Supper.

The gesture of giving the place of honor to Judas was Jesus' attempt to try to reach this man's heart. Another mark of honor which Jesus bestowed was the giving of this little morsel. It was a custom of the Jews to break off a piece of bread or a bit of meat, dip it in juice, and hand it to a favored guest—much as we propose a toast in someone's honor at a banquet today. Jesus took the bread and dipped it in the gravy and gave it to Judas in the presence of all the disciples. Only John heard Jesus say that this would mark the betrayer. So, when Jesus gave this morsel to Judas he was honoring him in the presence of the other disciples.

Yet never once in all the times that Judas was with Jesus is there any record that he ever relented and allowed Jesus to love him. He never opened up, never admitted what he was thinking. He never responded to Jesus' love in the least degree, but instead, kept up a false front, a phony facade. Now at last, despite the efforts of Jesus to reach him, he "lifted up his heel" against him and kicked him right in the face. So we come to the last step of this tragic sequence, showing the increasing grip of evil on Judas:

> *Then after the morsel, Satan entered into him.*
> *Jesus said to him, "What you are going to do,*
> *do quickly." Now no one at the table knew why*
> *he said this to him. Some thought that, because*
> *Judas had the money box, Jesus was telling*
> *him, "Buy what we need for the feast"; or, that*
> *he should give something to the poor. So, after*
> *receiving the morsel, he immediately went out;*
> *and it was night.*   John 13:27-30

You remember that the chapter began with the record of satanic influence upon Judas. In verse 2, John says: *And during supper, when the devil had already put it into the heart of Judas Iscariot, Simon's son, to betray him.* There we see that Judas's greed had given the devil an opportunity. When we resist God's love and follow a determined march toward evil, it gives the devil opportunity. He had the opportunity to implant thoughts which would immediately take deep root in Judas's heart. He had already put it into Judas's heart to betray Jesus; the deal had been arranged.

Beyond Hope

But Judas still has a chance to retreat. Jesus would never have tried to reach him had he not still had an opportunity to recover at this point. But when Jesus gives him the morsel, and Judas takes it and eats it without a word or a sign of repentance or remorse he passes the point of no return. This is one of the most tragic scenes in all of history—to see a man, while he is still alive, deliberately reject truth to the extent that he goes beyond any hope of recovery. At this point Satan enters into him, and now Judas is no longer in control of his will, but is possessed by Satan; he can no longer make any decision to resist evil. He is in the grip of death.

This is what we might call Judas's Gethsemane. Right after this event Jesus leaves the Upper Room and goes with his disciples into the Garden, where he withdraws a bit, and prays alone. This is his last chance to turn back before the cross. You remember that he prays: *My Father, if it be possible, let this cup pass from me;* but he adds, as always: *Nevertheless, not as I will, but as thou wilt* (Matthew 26:39). And though he sweats great drops of blood in the agony of that moment, we read that at the end of it an angel comes and strengthens him (*see* Luke 22:42-44). His resolve is unbroken. Similarly, the Upper Room is the moment when Judas is at the point of no return. It is his last chance to turn back, but he doesn't take it. When he makes his decision, Satan comes and strengthens him, so that he cannot turn back.

So Jesus commands him, now that there is no further hope of recovery: *What you are going to do, do quickly!* And the final word of John on this point is: *He immediately went out; and it was night.* John very likely is thinking in the same terms as the words he later would write in his First Epistle: *If we walk in the light, as he is in the light....* [if we walk out where our lives are open, where we don't try to hide anything, where our sins and our failures and our

weaknesses are all there before God, and we don't try
to justify or hide them, but we expose them] ... *the
blood of Jesus his Son cleanses us from all sin* (1 John
1:7). But if we turn from the light, turn our backs on
Jesus and walk away, determined to do our own will,
we walk into darkness, into night. It is Jude, one of
the brothers of Jesus, who later records that there are
those who are like *wandering stars for whom the
nether gloom of darkness has been reserved forever*
(Jude 13).

The Principle of Glory

So Judas leaves, and Jesus now turns to his disciples. Now he shares with them great truths that he
was unable to share while the traitor was present:

> *When he had gone out, Jesus said, "Now is the
> Son of man glorified, and in him God is glori-
> fied; if God is glorified in him, God will also
> glorify him in himself, and glorify him at once.
> Little children, yet a little while I am with you.
> You will seek me; and as I said to the Jews so
> now I say to you, 'Where I am going you cannot
> come.' A new commandment I give to you, that
> you love one another; even as I have loved you,
> that you also love one another. By this all men
> will know that you are my disciples, if you have
> love for one another."*   John 13:31-35

Here in this brief passage is the key to the rest of this
discourse. Chapters 14 through 17 all flow out of these
words. Jesus states an old principle, and gives a new
commandment. The old principle is in these words:
*Now is the Son of man glorified, and in him God is
glorified; if God is glorified in him, God will also glorify him in himself, and glorify him at once.* Notice the
stress on glory. The secret of glory, the principle by
which we achieve glory, is in the recognition of who we
really are. Glory is something we all long for and strive
for. We want to be recognized; we want people to know
us. We long to be seen, to become the center of attention.
We all want people to think highly of us. That is what
Jesus is talking about. The secret of attaining this, he

says, is to give yourself up, to lose yourself. He is looking ahead to the cross. The cross became a practical
certainty the minute Judas left the room, and Jesus
says: *Now* [in view of this cross] *is the Son of man
glorified.*

Grace and Truth Revealed

Notice the three manifestations of glory in this sen-
tence. First, Jesus is glorified in the cross. The cross
is now so certain that in the rest of this passage he
speaks of it as though it is already accomplished. And
in the cross, the inner character of Jesus becomes visible. Remember that in the opening of this Gospel,
John says: *And the Word became flesh and dwelt
among us, full of grace and truth; we have beheld his
glory, glory as of the only Son from the Father* (John
1:14). All that fullness of grace and truth which was
his glory becomes visible in the cross.

As you look at the cross, and at all the circumstances
of the events surrounding it, you see the reality of
Jesus' humanity. There is the agony in the Garden of
Gethsemane—that strange, mysterious agony of spirit
when Jesus is so troubled, so distressed, that he sweats
great drops of blood and cries out in terrible, an-
guished cries to his Father. And there are his cries
from the cross—of thirst, of pain, of being forsaken—
all of these tell us that he is one with us. The noted
London preacher, W. E. Sangster, has written these
very appropriate words:

It is well that we should think, sometimes, of the Upper Room,
and of the Last Supper, and of his soul "exceeding sorrowful
unto death"; of Gethsemane, the deep shadow of the olive trees,
his loneliness, prayer, and disappointment with his disciples,
his bloody sweat; the traitor's kiss, the binding, the blow in the
face, the spitting, the buffeting, the mocking, the scourging,
the crown of thorns, the smiting; the sorrowful way, and the
burdensome cross, the exhaustion and collapse; the stripping,
the impaling, the jeers of his foes, the flight of his friends; the
hours on the cross, the darkness, his being forsaken of God; his
thirst, and the end.

In the story of that cross you can see the humanity of
his person, yet you can also see the serenity of his

faith. How fearless he was before Pilate! He said to
him: *You would have no power over me unless it had
been given you from above* ... (John 19:11). How
fearless he was before Herod—he stood silent, and
would not answer him—and before Caiaphas, the high
priest! How masterfully he directed these events! Also
on the cross we see the compassion of his love. He forgave the revolutionary beside him, and prayed for his
enemies. Previously, in the high priest's hall, he had
looked at Peter with compassion when Peter had denied him (*see* Luke 22:54-72). See the love and concern of his heart as he makes provision for his mother
—the last thing he does before he died—committing
her into the hands of John (*see* John 19:26, 27).

Finally there is that strange, unfathomable mystery
of his work—how he could be at once the sacrifice
being offered, and the priest offering the blood before
the Father. How could he be the victim of man's sin,
of man's hatred and cruelty and guilt and, at the same
time, the victor over all the forces of darkness and hell
and death, over the principalities and powers whom he
took and nailed to the cross? We never can fully understand it, but that is the glory of Jesus—his humanity,
his serenity, his compassion—all revealed in the cross
of Christ. The cross revealed his glory.

Then God was glorified in him. The cross not only
reveals Jesus, but it reveals the Father—the truth
about the Father. The strange idea has arisen among
Christians that Jesus was an innocent sufferer, placat-
ing the wrath of a terribly angry God who was ready
to smite humanity. But that is not the biblical view.
The Bible says: *God was in Christ reconciling the
world to himself* ... (2 Corinthians 5:19). We see in
the cross the holiness and the justice of God. Isaiah
says: *Yet it was the will of the Lord to bruise him; he
has put him to grief; when he makes himself an offering for sin* ... (Isaiah 53:10). There we see the power
and the sovereignty of God. Peter, on the day of Pentecost, could say: *Jesus* [was] *delivered up* [to be cruci-
fied] *according to the definite plan and foreknowledge
of God* ... (Acts 2:23). God was in charge of the
events. The cross reveals the mercy and love and grace
of the Father. As Paul writes to the Romans: *He who*

*did not spare his own Son but gave him up for us all,
will he not also give us all things with him?* (Romans
8:32).

Losers Will Be Keepers

So, as Jesus says, he is glorified, the Father is glorified, and God will glorify him again, and will do it immediately. Here he is thinking of his resurrection and
exaltation. Our Lord is declaring a great principle
here. How do you achieve glory? How do you achieve
the fulfillment you are wanting? The answer is: By
dying. *He who finds his life will lose it, and he who
loses his life for my sake* [Jesus said] *will find it*
(Matthew 10:30). For after death is resurrection—the
exaltation of God. Peter puts it precisely in his First
Epistle: *Humble yourselves therefore under the mighty
hand of God, that in due time he may exalt you* (1 Peter
5:6).

That is difficult for the natural man. We struggle
with this. We fight for the top place. We are filled with
suspicion and guile toward one another. We all want to
read each other's mail, to find out what is going on
in other people's lives—especially if they are in any
sense our rivals. How can we die then? How can we
lose our lives? What is the power that can make us be
willing to throw it all away, to give it all up?

That power that makes sacrifice possible is in the
new commandment. Jesus immediately adds: *A new
commandment I give to you, that you love one another;
even as I have loved you.* Dying cannot be done on any
other terms. Ambition is not enough. Love only suf-
fices. The key is in the phrase, *as I have loved you.*
That phrase is both the measure and the origin of our
love. Our love for one another, Jesus says, is to be
like his love for us. That is, we must love as he does,
without condition, ready to forgive, honest and candid,
open and acceptant toward each other. That is the
measure of it.

But then our love must originate from his love for
us. The Father loved the Son, and as he lived by that
love, so we are to live by the love of Jesus available to
us. We are to draw upon his loving acceptance of us in

order to reach out in loving acceptance to others, whether they are lovely or not.

Jesus himself says that this is the mark of true discipleship. "Do you want people to believe your message? They will when they see the mark. And this is the mark by which the world will know that you really are my disciples—because you reach out in love like this to each other. If you can't reach out like that in love, if you can't put another's need ahead of your own, and give up your own interests to minister to that need, then you are not my true disciples; you have no part with me."

Betrayal Versus Denial

The closing scene between Peter and Jesus reveals the essential difference between Judas and Peter.

Simon Peter said to him, "Lord, where are you going?" Jesus answered, "Where I am going you cannot follow me now; but you shall follow afterward." Peter said to him, "Lord, why cannot I follow you now? I will lay down my life for you." Jesus answered, "Will you lay down your life for me? Truly, truly, I say to you, the cock will not crow, till you have denied me three times."   John 13:36-38

Judas betrayed Jesus and Peter denied his Lord. What is the difference between these two men, between betrayal and denial? Jesus himself has already explained this for us in verse 10 of this chapter. Remember that he said Peter had *already* been bathed and needed only to wash his feet. Judas had *never* been bathed, had never opened up to the cleansing of love, and had never given his life to Jesus. Peter had dirty feet but a clean heart; Judas had an evil heart of unbelief, though perhaps an outward appearance of morality. That is always the sort of man who will betray Jesus.

What Peter lacked was an understanding of love. Peter thought he loved Jesus, and he did—with all the human emotion of which he was capable. But he had not yet learned to walk by the love of Christ. He had not yet learned that his strength was to be found not in his efforts to try to be something in himself, but in the love of Jesus for him. That is the secret of strength. Jesus knew that. Peter, with the utmost dedication of his flesh, with complete consecration and sincerity of heart, could say to Jesus, "Lord, I know where you're going—you're going into death. And I'll lay down my life for you." But Jesus understood. He said, "Peter, thank you. But before the cock crows (i.e. before the morning breaks) you will have denied me three times." That is how much his fleshly dedication was worth.

Remember though, the story at the close of John's Gospel, when Jesus gathered with his disciples on the shore of Galilee after the resurrection. He had built a fire for them, and laid on some fish to cook, and they had breakfast together. While they were eating, Jesus said to Peter, "Peter, do you love me?" And Peter said, "Lord, you *know* I love you." And twice again, "Peter, do you love me?" And Peter said, "Lord, you know everything. You know that now I love you." It was on this occasion that Jesus said, "Peter, feed my sheep" (*see* John 21:9—17). He commissioned him when Peter learned what true love really is. When he learned how to draw upon the available love of Jesus to strengthen him in order to reach out in love for others, then Jesus sent him out with a worldwide commission to feed the sheep of God.

In this account, John helps us to see how thoroughly Jesus knows us, understands us, and sees all that is going on in our lives, and is ready to impart to us the great secret by which we can fulfill his impossible demand—to give up in order to gain, to lose in order to win, to go down to defeat in order to arise as a victor. When we learn to love by the love of Jesus, and to draw upon him, then: *By this all men will know that you are my disciples.*

Lord, teach us to love in this way. We know that the principle of life out of death can never be fulfilled in us until we have learned the new commandment—to love one another as you have loved us. Teach us that, Lord. We stand, like Peter, uncertain, afraid, knowing that our human love can never stand the pressure and the test, but knowing, Lord, that you are able to say to us, as you said to Peter, "You cannot follow me now; but afterward you will." In Jesus' name. Amen.

3

The Cure for Troubled Hearts
John 14:1-11

As our Lord looked at his disciples he knew what was going on in their minds and hearts, knew how disturbed and upset they were, and knew what was causing it. He knew the remedy for it, as well, and this passage opens with his words to them:

> *Let not your hearts be troubled; believe in God,*
> *believe also in me.*   John 14:1

There are many among us who are suffering from the same affliction as were these disciples: troubled hearts, fearful hearts, upset, disturbed, agitated hearts. Our Lord knew that these men were afraid—afraid of what was coming. They were afraid of death, afraid that they, with him, were going to be executed by the Jews. They knew of the opposition which had developed against them in Jerusalem, the bitter hatred of the Pharisees and their determination to eliminate Jesus and all his disciples. They knew they were in danger, and so their hearts were deeply troubled as they gathered here with him.

But more than physical danger to themselves, his words about leaving them had struck terror into their hearts. They were afraid that even though they might escape death, they would have to go on living without him, and that was unbearable to them. They could bear to die with him; they could not bear to live or die without him. So as he gathers with them he says these words to them: *Let not your hearts be troubled.*

At a time when I was experiencing a period of this kind of heart trouble myself—distress of heart—I thought of these words, and they came home to me with tremendously new significance. I saw something in that simple phrase: *Let not your hearts be troubled* which I had never seen before. What impressed me were the words, "Let not." They mean that these disciples could do something about their problem. They held in their own hands the key to their release from heart trouble. It was possible for them either to let it happen, or *not* to let it happen. Our Lord is saying this to all of us; there is a way out of heart difficulty—this distress and fear concerning both death and life.

The remedy for heart trouble is contained in the two phrases which follow: . . . *believe in God, believe also in me.* Believe in God who is still in control, who knows what he is doing, who is capable of exercising infinite wisdom, infinite power, and infinite love—and believe in me, as the Guide who is made available to you. That is the secret. We will see how our Lord strove to impress anew upon the hearts of his disciples the fact that something was hidden in the remarkable relationship between him and his Father. *Believe in God, believe also in me.* For between the Father and the Son there is a relationship which is so important, so fundamental, that everything else will grow out of it. The rest of the chapter is built around this great secret.

Based upon this relationship our Lord promises to end their fears by coming to them again. Their basic fear was that he was going to leave them, and then they would have to face death *and life* without him. His reassuring word is, "I am not going to leave you, I am coming to you again."

You will understand this chapter more fully if you realize two facts. First, the Lord promises to come again in person to end their fear of death, so that death need hold no terror for them (as it need hold none for us). This assurance he gives them in the promise contained in verse 3. Second, he is going to come again by the Spirit to end their fear of life. He promises to be with them in all the difficulties and problems of their lives—in a living relationship similar to his relationship with the Father. That is stated flatly in verse 18: *I will not leave you desolate* [the word means orphans]; *I will come to you.* Both of these comings are made possible by that strange rela-

tionship which our Lord had with his Father, and
which lead him to say to these disciples: *Believe in
God, believe also in me.*

Now the answer to fear is faith. The next time you
are afraid, reach out for a promise of God, and lay
hold of it by the power of Jesus, and your fear will
vanish. There is no other answer to fear. Anything
else will permit the fear to come back again and again.
But the promise of God remains steady and sure, and
the availability of the resources of Jesus to lay hold
of it provides the way of deliverance.

Jesus' promise, then, to come and put an end to the
fear of death is found in these words:

> *In my Father's house are many rooms; if it were
> not so, would I have told you that I go to prepare
> a place for you? And when I go and prepare a
> place for you, I will come again and will take
> you to myself, that where I am you may be also.*
> **John 14:2, 3**

Our Lord is looking into the future with his disciples.
Here he unveils the nature of the future beyond death,
beyond this life. I don't think there is anyone who
hasn't at one time or another sensed the fear of what
lies in the unknown, beyond death. We have all felt
that strange solemnity of spirit which comes when we
confront the fact of death, the fact that we are all some
day going to die, and that our loved ones will die. Life
here must end, and what lies beyond? This is what our
Lord is facing here with his disciples.

My Father's House

He reassures them with four revelations about that
future. First, he states that what happens is going to
be within the Father's house. Of course, he is talking
to them as believers. They belong to him, and on that
basis he assures them: *In my Father's house are many
rooms.* What do you think he means by *my Father's
house?* Since this is the only time that phrase is em-
ployed in the New Testament, it is very difficult to say
exactly what it means by trying to compare it with
other passages—until you go to the Old Testament.

There you see that some of the prophets clearly in-
dicate that God dwells in the universe. The whole universe is the Father's house. God, speaking through the
Prophet Isaiah, says:

*Heaven is my throne and the earth is my foot-
stool; what is the house which you would build
for me, and what is the place of my rest? All
these things my hand has made, and so all these
things are mine....*   Isaiah 66:1, 2

On many occasions our Lord has been out with his
disciples under the brilliant sky at night. And as they
looked up into the heavens and saw the stars and galax-
ies whirling in space, he must have reminded them
many times that this was the Father's house.

I am often asked, "Does the Bible say anything
about whether there is life on other planets?" The
answer is that it doesn't, specifically. But hidden in
this reference there is a suggestion, I believe, that this
is the case. What Jesus says here is, "In my Father's
house are many *abiding places*." It should not be translated "mansions," as it is inaccurately interpreted in
the King James Version. It is not even "rooms," as
used in the Revised Standard Version. It is, literally,
"places to live"; it should read: *in my Father's house
are many places to live*. Earth is one place to live; this
is our address. But God has other addresses elsewhere.
What is happening in these other places out in the vast
universe around us is hard to say. But Jesus assures
us that there is an abundance of places to live, plenty
of them. Therefore, there is room in the Father's
house.

Second, he assures us that this is a certain revelation. I like the rendering of the King James Version
here. It is more in line with what the Greek is saying:
... if it were not so, I would have told you. That verse
has been a comfort to me many times. People often
say to me, "You know, Jesus said many things which
were simply an accommodation to the way people
thought in his day. He didn't try to correct everything,
but instead he reflected their errors." I think this verse
stands as a clear refutation of that argument. Jesus

said: *If it were not so, I would have told you.* That is, "I have come to correct the thinking of men, to set right their delusions, to reveal the ways in which they have been wrong, to straighten out their twisted, distorted ideas."

A Place for Us

Third, he says: *I go to prepare a place for you.* Now I don't fully know what that means. I don't think anyone does. But it indicates that there is a need for preparation of some sort. I am impressed with what the Apostle Paul tells us—that the Creation, including not only this planet and this solar system but the entire universe in all its vast complexity, is in the grip of a remorseless law which science calls "the second law of thermodynamics," the law of entropy, the law of decay, or as Paul calls it in Romans 8:20, the law of futility.

Creation is in the grip of futility—it is running down, its energy is being transposed into a form in which it is no longer available. It is like a great clock, once wound up, which is gradually running down, but which will become a new heaven and a new earth, built on entirely different principles. Perhaps that is what Jesus has in mind when he says to his disciples: *I go to prepare a place for you.* He left to reverse the law of entropy somewhere. At any rate, it was necessary for him to do this. He came to prepare *them* for heaven; he left to prepare *heaven* for them.

He Won't Send an Angel

This takes us into the specific promise of his coming again: *I will come again and will take you to myself, that where I am you may be also.* Notice the elements of that promise. First of all, it is a certain coming. "If I go and prepare a place for you, I *will* come again." Did he go? Yes, history is unanimous. The record shows that he went away. The tomb is empty. There is no grave of Jesus Christ anywhere on earth. He has gone away. And if he goes away, he says, just as certainly he will come again.

Do you remember how the angels underscored that fact in the account of the Ascension in the opening chapter of Acts? The disciples were gazing up into heaven as Jesus was ascending and when he disappeared from sight, hidden by a cloud, suddenly two men in white robes were standing there. They said to the disciples: *Why do you stand looking into heaven? This Jesus . . . will come in the same way as you saw him go into heaven* (Acts I:II). This is an amplification of Jesus' promise here: *If I go away, I will come again.* Everywhere in Scripture this coming again of Jesus Christ is referred to as the hope of the world.

And our Lord further reveals that it will be a personal return. He *himself* will come again. He isn't going to send an angel nor anyone else; he personally will return. And it will involve a departure of the saints, of his own, to be with him. *I will take you to myself, that where I am you may be also.* In the coming of the Spirit, which Jesus mentions later, Jesus comes to the believer, and the believer receives him to himself. But in this verse it is the other way around. He comes to the believers and takes them to be with him. Here, then, is a clear distinction between the two comings of Christ. This is the coming which Paul must have been thinking of when he wrote to the Christians at Thessalonica:

> *For the Lord himself will descend from heaven with a cry of command, with the archangel's call, and with the sound of the trumpet of God. And the dead in Christ will rise first; then we who are alive, who are left, shall be caught up together with them in the clouds to meet the Lord in the air; and so we shall always be with the Lord.*   1 Thessalonians 4:16, 17

Paul's words echo these words of Jesus: *I will take you to myself, that where I am you may be also.*

Out of Time—Into Eternity

What an answer that is, not only to the problems of history, but also to the personal fear of a believer facing death! Other passages make clear that this event, which is yet to break into history—the return of Jesus for his own—is the very event which every believer experiences when he dies. When we step out of time and into eternity we step into the coming of Jesus for his own. This, then, is the hope and the experience of everyone who dies as a member of the body of Jesus Christ. What an answer this is to the fear of death!

So many Christians seem to echo the fear and pessimism and despair of the world when they think of death as a somber, gloomy occasion. Rather, it ought to be a time of triumph and of joy, because a believer has gone home to be with the Lord.

I remember listening years ago to a radio broadcast of the "Bible Study Hour," when Dr. Donald Grey Barnhouse, pastor of a church in Philadelphia, was the speaker. I'll never forget his telling of the occasion when his first wife had died. After the funeral service, as he was driving his motherless children home, they were naturally overcome with grief at the parting. Dr. Barnhouse said that as he was trying to think of some word of comfort to give them, a huge moving van passed them and the shadow of the truck swept over the car. As the truck pulled on in front of them, an inspiration came to Dr. Barnhouse. He said, "Would you rather be run over by a truck, or by its shadow?" The children said, "Well, of course, Dad, we'd much rather be run over by the shadow! That can't hurt us at all." Dr. Barnhouse said, "Did you know that two thousand years ago the truck of death ran over the Lord Jesus in order that only its shadow might run over us?" And he went on to explain how David had said in the Twenty-Third Psalm: *Even though I walk through the valley of the shadow of death, I will fear no evil; for thou art with me (see v. 4)*. This is the promise which every believer has from the lips of Jesus himself: *I will come again and will take you to myself, that where I am you may be also.*

If You Know Me, You Know the Way

Then he goes on in the remaining verses to show us the way—the way to the Father, the way in which all this will be accomplished. And it all related to those remarkable words with which he began: Believe in God, believe also in me. He says to them: *And you know the way where I am going* (John 14:4).

*Thomas said to him, "Lord, we do not know
where you are going; how can we know the
way?" Jesus said to him, "I am the way, and the
truth, and the life; no one comes to the Father,
but by me. If you had known me, you would
have known my Father also; henceforth you
know him and have seen him."*   John 14:5-7

Here is the way to the Father at death, or the way to
the Father in the midst of life, for the secret of both is
found in this passage. I believe that Jesus deliberately
made this statement to these disciples in order to bring
to their knowledge something which they hadn't re-
alized. He said to them, "You *know* the way where I am
going." And Thomas, dear old "honest Thomas" (we
should never call him "doubting Thomas"; he was
simply too honest to say that he knew something which
he didn't realize he knew) said to him: *Lord, we do not
know where you are going; how can we know the way?*
But Jesus had said that they *did* know. And the truth
is, they did! They knew *him.* But they didn't *know*
that they knew.

Do you remember those distinctions we used to make
between the four classes in school? Freshmen, we were
told, are those who know not, and know not that they
know not. Sophomores are those, having advanced a
little, who know not, but know that they know not.
Juniors, on the other hand, are those who know, and
know not that they know. And seniors are supposed to
be those who know, and know that they know.

On that basis, Thomas and the other disciples here
are classified as juniors in the school of faith. And
Jesus is making clear to them that they know the way.
Thomas shook his head, "No, Lord, we don't know the
way. We don't even know where you're going." And
Jesus said, *"I am the way,* and the truth, and the life.
That's what I meant, Thomas. You know me; there-
fore you know the way. For I am the way."

Here is this unique and most remarkable claim of
Jesus. How it reveals the grandeur of his character and
being! In this inclusive statement Jesus relates all
things to the Father. "I am the way to the Father,"
he says. If you come to know Jesus, he will bring you

to God. As Peter puts it: *He will bring you to the knowledge of the Father.*

When I began my Christian life as a boy, many years ago now, my awareness of the One with whom I was dealing was that of the Lord Jesus. He filled my horizon. I remember how I loved the hymns which sang of the cross and of the work of Christ, and I loved to think about him as the Saviour, the One who redeems. But as I have lived as a Christian, gradually the Father has come into focus. More and more my thoughts are drawn to the Fatherhood of God, and I revel in the glory of that relationship, in the closeness of my sonship with the Father.

This is what Jesus says. He is the way to the Father. He brings you to the Father. You know the Father through him, for he is also the truth about the Father —as Paul puts it, *the truth as it is in Jesus.* All the knowledge of God which we human beings hunger for is revealed in the words of Jesus about the Father. He unveils the Father's heart, what kind of a Father he is—his power and his wisdom and his love. He is the life of the Father. That is a most amazing claim! The Father has given all life into his hands, so that he may give it to whomever he will. This is Jesus' claim, recorded in the fifth chapter of John. Only those who come to the Father by the Son can receive life. Matthew tells us: *. . . no one knows the Father except the Son and any one to whom the Son chooses to reveal him* (Matthew 11:27).

This fully meets the need of man. Jesus is the way, in order that the will of man may choose it; he is the truth, in order that the mind may comprehend it; he is the life, in order that the heart of man can experience it. Thus, to know Christ involves the whole man and leads to the full expression and experience of the fullness of God.

Truth Is Narrow-minded

But note also the exclusiveness of his claim: *"No one comes to the Father, but by me."* Every now and then I run into somebody who says, "You Christians are so bigoted, so narrow. Why do you insist that Jesus is the only way by which you can come to God? Other

religions have *their* ways; other religions are striving
to know the same God, and other religions are more
tolerant; but you Christians are so narrow!" And I
have to say, "That is true, we are narrow. At that
point Jesus himself was narrow, and we dare not go
beyond what he said because truth itself is narrow."

Have you ever thought how narrow the telephone
company is? If you want to call somebody up, the
phone company insists that you use a certain series of
numbers in exactly the proper sequence, and it leaves
absolutely no room for you to play around. It is utterly
narrow-minded at that point! Truth is that way. Jesus
is the fulfillment of his own word: *For the gate is
narrow . . . that leads to life, and those who find it are
few* (Matthew 7:14). Others may teach about God.
They may say that they teach the truth and seek the
life. But only Jesus says, "I *am* the way, I *am* the
truth, I *am* the life."

Jesus' words in verse 7: *If you had known me, you
would have known my Father also,* do not mean that
his disciples didn't know him. He is simply saying, "To
know me is to know my Father; henceforth you know
him and have seen him." That statement caused Philip
to break out in an unpremeditated cry:

*"Lord, show us the Father, and we shall be sat-
isfied." Jesus said to him, "Have I been with you
so long, and yet you do not know me, Philip?
He who has seen me has seen the Father; how
can you say, 'Show us the Father'? Do you not
believe that I am in the Father and the Father
in me? The words that I say to you I do not
speak on my own authority; but the Father who
dwells in me does his works. Believe me that I
am in the Father and the Father in me; or else
believe me for the sake of the works themselves."*
John 14:8-11

In this paragraph our Lord is dealing with the secret
of his own being. In some ways this is the most profound revelation that we have in the entire New Testament about the nature of the Lord's relationship
with the Father. And it is absolutely fundamental.

What he meant when he said to his disciples at the
beginning of this chapter: *Believe in God, believe also
in me,* was this: "Understand that there is a unique
relationship which is the secret of my life, and which
will be the secret of your life, too. You must understand that I have not come here simply to demonstrate how *God* works, how God looks, how God acts;
I have come to demonstrate how *a man* acts who is in
right relationship with God, who is filled with God.
The Father dwells in me, and he does the works. I do
them, but I do them by a secret relationship in which,
though I perform them—my mind thinks, my hands
work, and my body acts—it nevertheless is really the
Father who is doing all this through me. I live in him;
he lives in me."

He says to Philip, "If you want proof of this, look
at two things: my words, and my works. My words
prove that I am in the Father. I could never say what
I say if I were not in the Father, for what I say is
truth; it is reality, it is the way things are. And my
works prove that the Father is in me. A man could
never do what I do, but God can. And you must
understand this, Philip. Otherwise you will have no
understanding of the secret of your own life." For in
verse 20 he will go on to say: *In that day you will
know that I am in my Father, and you in me, and I
in you.*

In other words: "The relationship which I have
with the Father is the pattern for the relationship I
will have with you. Just as I live by means of the
Father at work in me, so you will live by means of me
at work in you. I will come to you; I will live in you,
I will work through you. And you can face every problem of life on that basis; I will be adequate to handle
anything that comes your way. Whatever life throws
at you of fear, of upset, of discouragement, of disappointment—whatever its nature may be—you can
handle it in the same way that I have handled life;
you in me, and I in you—as the Father is in me, and I
am in him."

Our Father, we thank you for this tremendous reassurance as we face the unknown. As we face death, as we face life, we have these marvelous words of Jesus to rest upon. "Let not your hearts be troubled. I will come again. I will come again at death; I will come again in life." And in all ways, Lord, this presence will be with us. We thank you for that. Help us to live on this basis today, in this present twentieth-century hour, and to demonstrate the quality of life that he lived. We ask in his name. Amen.

4

The Other Comforter
John 14:12-20

Jesus' relationship with his Father would be called, in modern terms, *his basic identity*. I don't suppose there is any more basic problem in human life than the need to discover who you are, to discover your identity. We hear a great deal these days about an identity crisis, and the need to find oneself. This reflects a tremendously important psychological fact. It is important to know who you are.

A friend was telling me recently that as he has grown older he has come to see how important it is to him to find out more about his father, to know and to understand him. You cannot really know who you are and what causes you to act the way you do without some knowledge of your heritage and the family from which you come. Many times the solution to your problems will lie in that discovery and you will come to understand yourself.

This is because *who you are* determines *what you do*. If what you do doesn't grow out of who you are, then you are living a fraud, a false life. You are putting up a front, a facade which is not real. You may think that you are getting away with it, but you're not! Somebody sees through that front, sees that it is false. This is a problem with our world, isn't it? It is true that we pass through identity crises, that we don't know who we are. And that is why Jesus is unveiling his identity to his disciples.

Jesus knows who he is, and he says it to the disciples again and again. As we have seen, everything he says and does grows out of a basic identity with his Father. He says: *Do you not believe that I am in the Father and the Father in me? (see John 14:10)*. That is the key. "My Father and I are together always. He works

48

in me, and I depend on him. That is the secret of life."
Then again in verse II he says: *Believe me that I am in
the Father and the Father in me.* This is the great
truth which needs to be apprehended, the revelation of
our Lord's own secret of identity.

It will help us to pick up the train of his logic if we
move on to verses 18 through 20 and then return to
the intervening verses. Jesus says to his disciples:

> *I will not leave you desolate; I will come to you.
> Yet a little while, and the world will see me no
> more, but you will see me; because I live, you
> will live also. In that day you will know that I
> am in my Father, and you in me, and I in you.*
>   John 14:18-20

That is the secret of *our* identity as believers. The most
fundamental fact of our life as Christians is there:
you in me, and I in you.

Jesus says that he is not going to leave them as orphans. These men are frightened. They know that he is
going away. They remember the intimations he has
given that it will be by violence, by being taken and
beaten and ultimately crucified. And they are fearful—
not only for him but for themselves. But now he reassures them, "I'm not going to leave you orphans,
I'm not going to abandon you. I will come to you."

The Day of the Spirit's Coming

Obviously he is not talking here about his Second
Coming. His reference to that is in verse 3 where he
has said that he will come again and take them to
himself. At his Second Coming, John tells us, every
eye shall see him (*see* Revelation 1:7). But here is a
way of coming which the world will not see, but in
which the disciples will not only see him but live by
him: *Because I live, you will live also.*

I take that to be more than merely a reference to
his Resurrection, and the promise of our resurrection
some day. It is really a reference to his coming by the
Spirit, the result of which will be *you in me, and I in
you.* And that is to be the secret of our lives, as his

relationship with the Father was the secret of his life. Earlier, Jesus has told his disciples: *As the living Father sent me, and I live because of the Father, so he who eats me will live because of me* (John 6:57).

Notice how he develops this idea, he uses a phrase which he will use repeatedly throughout this discourse: *In that day.* . . . In what day? In the day when he comes again to them in this remarkable and unique way by which *they* know him and live by him, but which *the world* cannot see. He is speaking of a new day about to begin, a fresh dawn beyond the night of Crucifixion and death, beginning at his Resurrection, but continuing on. And it will be characterized by new knowledge on their part: . . . *you will know* [the Greek word means "know by experience"] *that I am in the Father, and you are in me, and I am in you.* This day, unquestionably then, is the day of the Spirit's coming, when they will be given a new identity.

I find Christians all over this country who do not understand this truth about their new life in Christ. The truth from which they get their identity is this fact: that Jesus is in them, and lives in them. It is to this fact that they should return whenever there are pressures and problems and difficulties and heartaches and troubles and demands made upon them, because it is from this fact that the secret of life will flow to them. That is why Jesus places it so centrally in this passage.

As we now know, the Day of the Spirit began on the day of Pentecost, when suddenly the Spirit of God was poured out upon these believers, and they became changed men. And that day is still with us. It began two thousand years ago and it hasn't ended yet. In fact, on the day of Pentecost, Peter stood up and bracketed its extremes—the events which would mark the beginning and the end of the Day of the Spirit.

It begins with the pouring out of the Holy Spirit, as prophesied by the Prophet Joel. Peter quotes that prophecy. He says, *But this is what was spoken by the prophet Joel*—this pouring out of the Spirit upon men. And it ends, he says, when: *The sun shall be turned into darkness and the moon into blood, before the day of the Lord comes* (see Acts 2:16-20 and Joel 2:28-32).

But in between is the age of the Spirit, the Day of the Spirit.

Profile of the Holy Spirit

As we work back through this passage, we can see that four tremendous characteristics of the Holy Spirit are outlined for us in Jesus' words:

> *If you love me, you will keep my command-*
> *ments. And I will pray the Father, and he will*
> *give you another Counselor, to be with you for*
> *ever, even the Spirit of truth, whom the world*
> *cannot receive, because it neither sees him nor*
> *knows him; you know him, for he dwells with*
> *you, and will be in you.*   John 14:15-17

First, the One who is coming would be another Counselor. The word translated "Counselor" is *parakletos*. It means "one who is called alongside of," one who will be your companion, your strengthener, your guide. In the King James Version it is translated "Comforter" —One who is with you to strengthen you, to fortify you. And this Spirit will be *another* Comforter. Another than whom? Who was the first Comforter? It was Jesus himself. Jesus had been their Counselor, their Comforter, their Strengthener. He was the One who had guarded them and kept them and empowered them and taught them. Now there would be another who would come, another of the same kind.

Later on in this discourse, Jesus says: . . . *I did not say these things to you from the beginning, because I was with you* (John 16:4). They didn't need to know these things then. But now, as he is going away, he tells them that he has provided another Counselor who will strengthen them and minister to them. So the primary mark of the ministry of the Holy Spirit is that he does with us what Jesus did with his own disciples—he strengthens us.

No More Illusions

The second characteristic is that he would be the Spirit of truth. What does that mean? Truth, of course, is reality. Truth is what exists, what really is there.

The Spirit of God has come into our lives to lead us to understand what is there. There are many illusions in life, things that we think are true but which aren't true at all, principles upon which we act, expecting certain results, which don't appear. But the Spirit of truth has come to help us to understand life as it really is, to dispel these illusions and strip off all the falseness. He is the unending foe of every pretense, of every fraud, and of every bit of phoniness.

As Jesus says a little later on, he will also reveal the secrets of God, the hidden facts about life that we desperately need to know in order to live. Paul develops that idea strongly in First Corinthians, where he tells us of the hidden wisdom, the deep things of God, which are so necessary, but which *eye has not seen nor ear heard,* and which *God has prepared for those who love him* (*see* 1 Corinthians 2:9). These are made known to us, he says, by the Spirit.

The third characteristic, Jesus says, is that the world cannot receive him. *The world* means all those who are what we would call secularists or humanists, those who try to look at life without making any provision for God or for God's operation; who think of life as consisting merely of what can be observed and learned and acted on; and who think they don't really need God in order to live. Our world is being rapidly secularized. Education is losing its Christian perspective and is taking on a wholly secular point of view. Those who hold that viewpoint, Jesus says, cannot know the deep wisdom of God, cannot find the secrets of life. That is why, if we are restricted to following completely secular philosophies, we will repeat the same mistakes over and over again, generation after generation.

It is by the revelation of the truth as it is in Jesus, disseminated through the church, that the world is given light in the midst of its darkness. And if the church is not preaching the truth which is in the Scriptures but, rather, is ignoring it, then the world is in unrelieved darkness and has no way out. That is why life gets worse and worse throughout the generations; why secular ideas and philosophies govern, but cannot solve our problems. The world cannot receive the Spirit of truth because it does not believe him, Jesus says. It doesn't see him or know him. It doesn't believe that a spiritual kingdom exists, and thus cannot know the great secrets of life.

The fourth characteristic, Jesus says, is that the Spirit would operate from within the believer: ". . . *you know him, for he dwells with you, and will be in you.*" The primary reference here undoubtedly is to his disciples. Jesus could never say that of us, nor of anyone, after the day of Pentecost. We don't have to go through a process in which the Spirit first is *with* us and then is *in* us. But these men did. At this point in their experience Jesus had been with them, and thus the Spirit of God was *with* them, because Jesus was filled with the Spirit. Everything he did was by means of the Holy Spirit who was *in* him, but *with* them. But now Jesus is going away, and when he goes he will send the Spirit. And the Spirit will come to be *in* them. Everything they do, then, they can do by the power of the Spirit living in them.

It Is Still Jesus

All this is introduced to us by a very startling statement with which our Lord caught the attention of the disciples:

> *Truly, truly, I say to you, he who believes in me will also do the works that I do; and greater works than these will he do, because I go to the Father. Whatever you ask in my name, I will do it, that the Father may be glorified in the Son; if you ask anything in my name, I will do it.*
> John 14:12-14

That is one of the most startling promises in the Scriptures, and many have puzzled over it. There are three things we need to notice in this passage. The first is the reason he gives for these greater works. It is *because I go to the Father.* What does he mean? Well, when he goes to the Father, he will send the Spirit. He says later: . . . *If I do not go away, the Counselor will not come to you* (John 16:7). He is referring again here to the coming of the Spirit. As the Spirit of God comes into human hearts and dwells in them,

these things will happen—by means of the Spirit. The
Spirit, of course, is releasing to us the life of Jesus,
so that it is still Jesus who is doing these things.

We need to understand that. Some people read this
passage and think that we ordinary human mortals,
living here in the twentieth century, are somehow
going to be so capable, so well developed, so intellect-
ually astute, that we can actually do greater things
than the Son of God himself did when he was here in
the flesh. That isn't what he says. He is telling us that
he will do greater things through us, as the risen Lord,
dwelling in us by means of the Spirit, than he did
when he was here in the days of his flesh. And, in
either case, it is *he* who is doing it.

Some time ago I attended a public breakfast meeting designed to emphasize the spiritual values of life.
It was one of those times when God seemed to come
down and meet each one of us. Even though there
were hundreds of non-Christians present, there was
still a deep sense of God's presence. At the close of the
meeting, I heard two men discussing it on their way
out. One said, "Well, God must have been very pleased
with this meeting." The other said, "Yes, he probably
was—he did it!" That captaures exactly what Jesus
means here. He is going to do it because he goes to
the Father and by that means sends the Spirit.

What Greater Things?

The result will be that *he who believes in me will also
do the works that I do.* Unquestionably this refers to
the miracles that he performed. But what does this
mean? Can Christians do miracles like Jesus did —
raise the dead, heal the sick, open the eyes of the blind,
still the storm, multiply the loaves and fishes—all these
great signs? The answer is yes. If you read the record
of church history you learn that there have been occasional manifestations of miracles of this nature. These
are well documented and cannot be denied. And this
same kind of power, by God's hand, is still at work
among us from time to time.

But the focus of this passage is not on these physical
miracles. Jesus drives on immediately to say: *And
greater works than these will you do.* Now, what are

they? Obviously they can't be greater miracles, because there are no miracles greater than his. Can you think of anything greater than opening the eyes of those born blind, or speaking a word and enabling a lame man to walk, or delivering the oppressed, or raising the dead? Can there be any greater miracles than those? Of course not. Then what are these greater works? The only answer that makes any sense at all is that they are greater in their significance and importance. In other words, they are *spiritual* accomplishments, rather than physical. Anything done to the spirit of man is far more significant than something done to the body. That is what Jesus is speak of.

As you read the account of his ministry, notice that although the crowds followed him when he did those amazing wonders, and entire cities would turn out to hear his message, yet when you come to the end of his life—when he is facing the cross—where are all the crowds who heard him? Where are the hundreds whom he must have healed? They are gone. Only a handful are found at the foot of the cross. By every human reckoning the ministry of Jesus was a total failure. His miracles did not change people; they merely touched the surface of their lives.

But later on in this account Jesus says to his disciples: *You did not choose me, but I chose you and appointed you that you should go and bear fruit and that your fruit should abide* . . . [your fruit will remain] (John 15:16). Isn't it interesting that the ones whom Jesus healed would not stand with him through the test of the cross, but that when these disciples went out and preached in the power of the Spirit they won converts by the thousands, all across the length and breadth of the Roman Empire. And when the testing came, these men and women—won by the preaching of these disciples—were willing to face lions, to endure torture, to be pulled apart on the rack, to be bound up in skin bags and thrown into the sea, to be burned as living torches, to be mangled and mashed and twisted and torn apart, rather than to deny Jesus? "*Your* fruit will remain."

Those are greater miracles, aren't they? Anything done to the spirit of man is permanent; that which is done to the flesh is merely temporary. All those whom Jesus healed or raised from the dead died again. There is no record of it, but Lazarus must have died again, even though Jesus raised him from the dead. They all died. So, what is done to the spirit of man is far greater, and this is what Jesus means by greater works.

A Qualified Promise

Finally, we come to his method, which is that of prayer. How will these things happen? He adds immediately:

> *Whatever you ask in my name, I will do it, that the Father may be glorified in the Son; if you ask anything in my name, I will do it.*
>
> John 14:13, 14

That is an amazing promise! We often read that without careful thought of the context, and we are seized by the tremendous possibilities of that word *anything*. And shallow, superficial Christians, their passions aroused, leap up and say, "Oh boy! What a promise! I can have that new Cadillac I've always wanted." But James reminds us: *You ask and do not receive, because you ask wrongly, to spend it on your passions* (James 4:3).

No, that isn't what it means. You see, there is a limitation to this promise and a very important one. It is obvious that it couldn't be taken in an unlimited sense, because it would be contradictory. What if somebody prays for rain because his crops need it, and somebody else prays for sunshine so that he can put a new roof on his house—whose prayer is answered? I remember hearing my dear friend, Dr. Howard Hendricks, tell of the time when he was a young man, before he was married. He was aware that certain mothers had set their caps for him on behalf of their daughters. One mother even said to him one day, "Howard, I just want you to know that I'm praying that you'll be my son-in-law." Dr. Hendricks always stops at that point in the story and says very solemnly, "Have you ever thanked God for unanswered prayer?"

What does it mean, then? Surely the words of Jesus
are not without meaning. What is the limitation here?
If you examine it you find only one, "Ask anything
whatsoever *in my name* and it shall be done." What
does that mean—*in my name?* Somehow again, in a
superficial approach to these ideas of Scripture, some
think they have fulfilled this when they tack on at the
end of a prayer, "This we ask in Jesus' name"—as a
kind of magic formula, like rubbing Aladdin's lamp so
that the "genie" of God will suddenly appear and do all
that we ask!

Now, I have no objection to people adding those
words. I do it myself. But there are many prayers with
those words tacked onto the end which are not prayed
in Jesus' name at all. To add those words does not
make it a prayer in Jesus' name. God is not impressed
with this kind of trivia. I think of our Lord's teaching about prayer in the Sermon on the Mount where
he says, "Don't pray like the hypocrites do, thinking
that you impress God with your endless repetition"
(*see* Matthew 6:5, 7). Prayer is not magic.

What, then, does "in Jesus' name" mean? I've been
given some difficult and painful lessons on what this
means! I think God teaches us through our experiences,
as we go on through life, to give us deeper and deeper
insight into what these phrases mean. I had thought
that praying in Jesus' name meant praying for the
things he wants accomplished, the ends he wishes to
achieve, the desires which he says are his will. And it
does mean that; that is not wrong. But I thought you
could pray to prevent certain things, and to attain
others, and that we had an ability somehow to control
the process by which these things come to pass. I have
learned that this is not the case. I prayed for weeks,
with all my heart, that something wouldn't happen,
but one day it did happen, in spite of my prayer.

Accept the Process of God

So what do you do with your prayer in a case like
that? And what do you do with the promise? I learned
that "in Jesus' name" means to pray *in his place*. That
is the way we use the phrase, isn't it? If someone acts
in the name of the president, it is as though he is

standing in the president's place. If you give someone the power to act in your name, for that purpose it is as though you yourself were acting. When you sign your name on a check, that check is acting on your behalf, as though it were you. To pray in Jesus' name means to stand in Jesus' place. And where was Jesus standing when he said these words? Facing the cross. Facing the collapse of all the hope that his kingdom had raised in the hearts of his disciples. Facing the end, the apparent collapse and failure of all of his work and all of his program.

But he knew that beyond the cross lay the Resurrection, and that there could never be that new beginning if there were not first an end of all which the others saw and hoped for. I think that if these disciples were praying for anything, and I'm sure they were, they were praying that somehow he would be spared, that somehow he would not have to go to the cross. They were praying to prevent it. But Jesus knew that it had to be. And to pray in Jesus' name means that you accept the process of God, the process by which he brings matters, often, to utter collapse, so that the very thing you don't want to ever happen, happens. But that is not the end of the story! Beyond it is a Resurrection. Beyond it is a new beginning, a beginning of such different quality that the mind moves into an ecstasy of joy in contemplating it. That is what it means to pray in Jesus' name.

That is why when we pray, it often seems as though God waits until the very last moment to answer our prayer. That is why he doesn't stop the process long before the heartache and pain comes, but allows it to go on into death—and out of the death comes Resurrection. And to pray in Jesus' name means that you consent to that process, and that you are aware that prayer is not merely a shield, a guard, to prevent things from happening. Sometimes it is, but not always. Prayer is also a commitment to undergo the end and the collapse and the failure. But that is never the end of the story. It is by this means that the greater works shall be accomplished. It is only out of death that life comes.

This is what God teaches us all through the Scriptures. This is why one day he had to say to Abraham, "Take your son Isaac, your only son, your beloved son, and offer him up as a sacrifice." And Abraham had to go through with it. It was only as the knife was poised in his hand, ready to plunge into the breast of his son, that God stopped him (*see* Genesis 22:1-12). The Book of Hebrews says that Abraham received his son back as though it were a Resurrection—out of death comes life (*see* Hebrews 11:19). That is what it means to pray in Jesus' name. It may mean, therefore, the collapse of all that you hoped for. But out of that collapse, out of the tears, out of the heartbreak, God will bring new life.

Our Father, we take some of these things of yours so shallowly, at times. We pray so glibly and without understanding. But we thank you that you teach us, Lord, again and again through life, that you are never going to deviate from your process. As Jesus taught us, "If any man will come after me, let him deny himself and take up his cross and follow me. For whoever would save his life will lose it, and whoever loses his life for my sake will find it." May we gladly consent to that process, Lord, in order that we may see the greater works which the world has not seen before —"greater works than these"—because, Lord Jesus, you have gone to the Father. We thank you in your name. Amen.

5
Love's Power
John 14:21-31

We now find ourselves in a section that includes some *precious and very great promises* (*see* 2 Peter 1:4). I hope we will gain considerable insight into the problem of obedience—especially what it is that motivates Christian obedience—and learn something of the riches of peace and joy which await the obedient heart.

The Lord Jesus has already given to his disciples the radiant secret of the Christian life. He has said: *In that day you will know that I am in my Father, and you in me, and I in you* (John 14:20). The day he speaks of, remember, is the Day of the Spirit, characterized by the indwelling of the Spirit within men and women everywhere—all kinds of people—producing the work of God in the human heart.

Now he goes on to speak about love and obedience:

He who has my commandments and keeps them,
he it is who loves me. . . . John 14:21

Notice carefully the connection between verse 21 and what we have just looked at in verse 20. Here you have the proof of love: "He who has my commandments and keeps them is the one who loves me," says Jesus.

The Love of Christ Constrains Us
But notice that he does not reverse this, as many do who read this. They think he says that if you obey him you will thereby love him, that obeying his commandments is what creates love for him. I find that there are a great many Christians who are trying to live on that basis, who exhibit in their lives a very mechanical obedience which they think will create love -for Christ. But instead, that is the recipe for

legalism. To read this, "Obey me, and you will love me," produces a mechanical, sterile, dry, dusty Christianity with no warmth or joy or glory.

But what Jesus says is, "If you love me, you will obey me." It is easy to do, not difficult. Look at verse 15 where he says this very plainly: *If you love me, you will keep my commandments.* Notice, it is not, "If you love me, you *must* keep my commandments." No, it is cause and effect: "If you love me, the result is that you *will* keep my commandments." That is the secret of all proper behavior in the Christian experience, and we need very carefully to make that clear. The proof of our love is obedience. That is how we demonstrate that we already love him.

Now, if it takes love to obey, what produces love? That is really the question, isn't it? That is the issue. If you see a Christian disobeying Christ or you yourself are tempted to disobey, what is it that will turn you around and make you obey? It is love. Well, how do you produce love? What will make you love him? This is what ties together these two verses. It is that basic secret of our identity which creates love. The Spirit in us, releasing to us the love of Jesus, awakens love from us in return. Remember how John puts it: *We love, because he first loved us* (1 John 4:19). Remembering this awakens love. Or, as Paul writes: . . . *God's love has been poured into our hearts through the Holy Spirit which has been given to us* (Romans 5:5).

Therefore, the way to produce love is to remember who you are, to whom you belong, and who Jesus is—his death, his resurrection, and his unity with you, his present indwelling life. You cannot remind yourself of that without experiencing a renewed sense of his love and of gratitude to him for who he is and what he has done in your life. And when that love begins to flow, then you are being motivated to obey.

Has it occurred to you that much of the mythology of the ancient world was based upon Christian truth, that fables and fairy tales are, in a sense, garbled and distorted versions of Christian fact? Some of our more modern fables are the same. You remember Clark Kent, that mild-mannered newspaper reporter, of whom no one ever expected anything out of the ordinary. But whenever there was a sudden demand for action far beyond the ability of mortal men, he stepped into the nearest phone booth (fortunately one was always handy), stripped off his conservative business suit, and emerged complete with bulging muscles and spectacular costume as—SUPERMAN—able to do what otherwise he could not do.

That is exactly what the Word of God is teaching us, although perhaps you had not seen it in those terms before! We are to retire to the "phone booth" of our identity with Christ, to remind ourselves of who we are, to whom we belong, and who is within us, and immediately we find love and motivation and power available to us. We are able to do what otherwise we could not do. This is what our Lord is teaching his disciples at this moment: *If you love me, you will keep my commandments.* When we love him, when we retreat to that place and love is made known in our hearts by the Spirit, obedience becomes much easier.

Therefore the key to motivation is not to threaten but to appeal. This is why Paul writes to Christians: *I appeal to you therefore, brethren, by the mercies of God, to present your bodies* ... (Romans 12:1). There *is* a place for fear as a motive in the Christian life, usually in terms of preventing us from doing what we ought not to do. When you are tempted to do something you know is wrong, fear comes in, and properly so— fear of God's just reprisal, of the consequences of your actions; fear of hurting others and of being hurt yourself; fear of having to stand before the searching eyes of God, knowing that he sees the utmost secrets of your life. Fear, then, keeps you from doing what is wrong. But when you are asked to do something which is right, what movtivates you then? Love. Love of is right, what motivates you then? Love. Love for Jesus.

Submission Is Not a Dirty Word

Have you noticed how many times in the Scriptures appeals are made to us to do what our flesh rebels at doing? To submit to authority, for instance. I come to a stop sign, and I'm in a hurry. The sign says STOP and I don't want to stop; I want to keep going. But to stop is part of my Christian life, because that is obedience to the authorities. Wives are to submit to their husbands, and they don't want to—especially in these days when a twisted form of liberation is being proclaimed. Some think the word *submit* is a dirty word, not realizing that it is a Christian word which applies to everybody—men, women, and children alike. Husbands are asked to submit to Christ and to his Word, and they don't want to do that. Servants are asked to submit to their masters, to yield them glad obedience. When somebody asks you to do something you know you ought to do, but you don't want to do it—your flesh wants to refuse, to say, "Hang it on your ear! Who do you think you are, telling me what to do?" What will motivate you to want to do it?

Have you ever noticed how many times in these passages you find little phrases like: *for the Lord's sake* or *out of reverence for Christ* or *as unto the Lord?* Why is this? Well, in such cases there is usually no fear of consequences to motivate you; it is out of love for Jesus that you are to do it. *For the Lord's sake* submit yourselves one to another—wives unto husbands, husbands unto wives, children unto parents. *For the Lord's sake*—do this because you love him.

Not by Bread Alone

I have never been able to understand how a person could claim to love Christ and yet deliberately disobey, knowing that he is being disobedient and refusing to follow the Lord. That is the name of the game—obedience—following the Lord, doing what he says. The proof of our love, therefore, is our obedience. When we obey we are demonstrating our love for the Lord. There are two elements of proof, our Lord says: *He who* [1] *has my commandments and* [2] *keeps them....* To have his commandments means to be exposed to his Word and know what it says. His words tell us what life is like, and what we are to do. To have them means not only to own a Bible but to read it, to study it, to learn it, to teach it. There are Christians who think they can live a Christian life without ever reading their Bibles, but it is impossible. Our memories do not retain and maintain what we need to know. We are built in such

a way that we need refreshment and reminder—again
and again.

I once went with a team of men to a series of meetings in the northwestern states. In city after city, as we
talked to pastors and laymen from scores of churches,
we began, as some would say, to "do a slow burn." We
become angrier and angrier because we were meeting
young people from all over the region who were crying
out for someone to teach them the Word of God—
teaching they were not finding in the churches of that
area of Canada.

Toward the end of the week we had a breakfast
meeting at which we set forth some of the essentials
necessary to health in the church—among them the
teaching of the Word of God. At the end of the meeting our host, a Canadian businessman who had traveled
with us faithfully all week, suddenly could stand it no
longer. He stood up and said to these pastors, "Look,
I'm not an American; I'm a Canadian. I have two sons
who have been seeking for some Bible teaching for a
long time. They were spiritually hungry and went from
church to church in this city, searching for a place
where the Word of God is expounded from the pulpit
... and found none. Finally they drifted into wrongful,
hurtful practices because they could find no one who
would expound the Scriptures to them." His voice
broke, and he could hardly control himself as he poured
out his heart to these pastors. He said, "Why, why will
you not teach the Word of God to people?" It was a
moving plea. And that is what Jesus means. Can we
not apply that to our own hearts and say, "Why will
we not read his Word? Why will we not spend some
time in learning what he says?"

The second element of proof is that he who has
Jesus' commandments keeps them. He follows them,
commits himself to obey what the Lord has said, to do
what he asks. *He who has my commandments and keeps
them, he it is who loves me.* If you want to convince
Jesus Christ that you love him, just obey him, that's
all. Just do what he asks. He will know that your obedience cannot come except out of a heart moved by
love for him.

The Reward of Love

Three things follow for those who love him—not merely believe in him, notice, but love him and thus obey him. Our Lord says:

He who has my commandments and keeps them, he it is who loves me; and he who loves me will be loved by my Father, and I will love him and manifest myself to him.   John 14:21

First, they will be loved by the Father. Isn't it remarkable that though we begin our Christian life at the feet of Jesus—we see him who is our Redeemer, our Saviour —it isn't very long before we are conscious of belonging to a family and being loved by a Father.

One of the men who went with us on our trip gave his testimony wherever we went. I was struck by his description of how empty his life had once been. Even though he was raised in a church and had known these Bible truths all his life, nevertheless his life was empty and unsatisfying—a wreck. Then he began to understand this great, basic secret of identity—*You in me, and I in you*—and he began to live on that basis. His problems were being solved, he told us, because he had a loving, heavenly Father who was at work to solve them. Being loved by the Father is evidenced through our circumstances. It is the discipline of God which puts us into various circumstances in order to train us and to teach us. He gives us joyful and happy circumstances as well as difficult and demanding ones. That is the expression of the love of the Father.

The second part of the reward, Jesus says, is—*I will love him*—and that is something different. The Father loves us by meeting our needs. His love is that of supply and training, whereas the Lord Jesus loves us by inward release to our feelings, through our sense of his being and of his love. The love of Jesus has more to do with our feelings than does the Father's love. Paul prays for the Ephesians; *that Christ may dwell in your hearts through faith; that you, being rooted and grounded in love* (Ephesians 3:17). That feeling of being accepted, of being important, of having worth as a human being, that sense of belonging to the Lord

Jesus himself—the knowledge and understanding of that is what he is speaking of here.

The third element of this reward of love is: *I will manifest myself to him.* That is, occasions and circumstances will arise in which Jesus will be very near, very real, very dear to you. Increasingly you will learn to know him and to enter into the understanding of the being and character of the Son of God. This speaks to the hearts of all who are Christians. The one thing we want more than anything else is a deeper knowledge of Jesus. This he promises to those who love him and thus obey him. He will manifest himself to them. There have been times in my own experience when the Lord Jesus has been more real to me than any other person —so real, it seemed, that I could touch him! This is the manifestation of his response to love from us.

Then Judas, one of the disciples, asks a question, out of which comes a remarkable answer:

Judas (not Iscariot) said to him, "Lord, how is it that you will manifest yourself to us, and not to the world?"   John 14:22

The Jews understood that when the Messiah came he would manifest himself to the whole world. But Jesus had said that he would manifest himself to these disciples in a way that the world could not perceive. Judas is curious about this and so he asks the question. In the answer Jesus gives, there are four elements which describe how he is going to do this, how he will manifest himself to us.

The Sweet and Tender Things
First he repeats what he said before:

Jesus answered him, "If a man loves me, he will keep my word, and my Father will love him, and we will come to him [then he adds this:] *and make our home with him."*   John 14:23

That is a beautiful phrase, isn't it? "Our home will be with him—we will live together." Out of the experi-

ence of life in God's family will come the sense of the
presence of Jesus. Probably all of us have had occasion
to be away from home—perhaps at Christmas—when
we would love to have been there. Memory then brings
to mind all the sweet and tender things, the little things
which make home such a wonderful place to be. I think
this is what our Lord has in mind. In many little ways,
in tender moments, in compassionate care, in ways of
comforting us and touching us, as a family lives and
shares life together, so this revelation of Jesus will
come. The manifestation of him will grow out of family life together.

Then he gives us the negative side:

> *He who does not love me does not keep my*
> *words; and the word which you hear is not*
> *mine but the Father's who sent me.*   John 14:24

There he puts his finger upon the secret of disobedi-
ence. If we are not following the Lord at some point,
why is it? The answer is that at that point, in that
area, *we do not love him.* In other ways and places we
do love him, but at that point we do not; we are denying
him, and do not love him. If we do not love him we will
not obey him, Jesus said. And what we are disobeying is
the Word of God. We are disobeying the Father as well
as the Son.

Then he goes on to the second element of manifestation:

> *These things I have spoken to you, while I am*
> *still with you. But the Counselor, the Holy Spirit,*
> *whom the Father will send in my name, he will*
> *teach you all things, and bring to your remem-*
> *brance all that I have said to you.*
>
> John 14:25, 26

First of all, it is very clear that the primary reference
here is to the apostles themselves. This is the explanation of how we got the Gospels and the Epistles. It is
true that they had memories of their time with Jesus,
but these recollections would have been a very faulty
thing to rely upon—if that were all they had. It is true

that there were certain written accounts which were
sometimes incorporated into the New Testament record. Luke, in particular, gathered some of them together and put them into his accounts. It is true that
they passed stories along from one to another. But
primarily, what accounts for the Gospels and Epistles
is the teaching of the Holy Spirit, the fact that when
the Spirit came, he brought to the apostles' memories
all the things Jesus said and did, and he taught them
all things. We can be grateful that we have the apostolic word undergirded by the inspiration of the Holy
Spirit, thus guaranteeing its accuracy.

But there is also a secondary application to our own
hearts. Have you ever been taught by the Holy Spirit?
Have you ever known a word of Scripture, perhaps for
a long time, and then gone through some circumstance
which caused that word to take on new, luminous meaning which it never had for you before? In the last
chapter, I mentioned how the phrase, "whatsoever you
ask in my name" came alive to me in a new way. I
began to see that it involves the cross and the resurrection, the process of death, and life out of death, I
had never seen it quite that way before. That is the
teaching of the Holy Spirit. He takes the circumstances of life and uses them to cause these words to
glow, to leap off the page, and burn themselves into
our hearts in a new and fresh way. By that means,
Jesus manifests himself to us, and we learn more of
what he is like.

Uncircumstantial Peace

The third element is the heritage of peace which is
ours:

> *Peace I leave with you; my peace I give to you;
> not as the world gives do I give to you. Let not
> your hearts be troubled, neither let them be
> afraid.*   John 14:27

Have you really come to understand the great fact that
peace is our inheritance? Peace is what Jesus has left
us. It is basic and fundamental and cannot be taken
away from us by any circumstance. That is what he

means by, "I give not as the world gives." How does the world give peace? If you were troubled, upset, and disturbed, and you went to a doctor who was not a Christian and asked him, "What can I do to gain peace?" what would he tell you? "Take a trip. Go to Hawaii. Get away from it all." In other words: "Change your circumstances. Get to the place where nothing bothers you, where everything is peaceful around you. Then you can be at peace."

But Jesus says, "I give peace right in the midst of trouble, right in the midst of distress and turmoil and heartache and pressure. I can impart peace to your heart right here, and not as the world gives." Why? Because we can return to that basic relationship we have—"You in me, and I in you." Out of that comes the guarantee that he is working out his purposes. *He* will bring us to the end of the trouble. *He* will still the storm and quiet the waves. We rest in the boat, content, knowing that "No water can swallow the ship where lies, the Master of ocean and earth and skies" (from "Peace, Be Still" by Mary A. Baker). That is peace.

Peace I leave with you. [Therefore], the Lord adds: *Let not your hearts be troubled.* That is addressed to you! It means you do not have to be upset and anxious, troubled and weary and worried. *Let not your hearts be troubled.* How? By returning to that place of rest. Return to the "phone booth" and rest there in the confidence that "Superman" is within and will work the situation out for you, and will do it through you. And he will! That is where your heart finds surcease from trouble.

The fourth element is his suggestion of the advantage we have over the apostles in the days of his flesh:

> *You heard me say to you, 'I go away, and I will come to you.' If you loved me, you would have rejoiced, because I go to the Father; for the Father is greater than I. And now I have told you before it takes place, so that when it does take place, you may believe.*   John 14:28, 29

When what takes place? Why, the coming of the Spirit.
Jesus is going away—in order that he might send the
Spirit. He is going to the Father, leaving the place of
his limitation, the circumstance in which the Father is
greater than he. When he says: *The Father is greater
than I*, he is referring, of course, only to his self-
imposed limitations in the days of his humiliation,
when he was here as a man. Don't misunderstand that.
The cults attempt to derive from this a theological
teaching that the Son is always less than the Father.
That is not so. The Son of God is equal with the Father,
as Paul tells us very plainly (*see* Philippians 2:6). But
for the moment, in the days of his flesh, in this restricted sense, the Father was greater than he. Now
he is returning to that status of equality in every sense
with the Father, which was his before the incarnation,
and he says, "You ought to rejoice, because I will send
the Spirit. And I will be nearer to you then than I am
now."

These men did not believe that. *We* have trouble
believing that. But they found it to be true. When the
Day of the Spirit came, there was an inner revelation
of Jesus which they had never known in the days of
his flesh. And he is saying this to us as well: "I will
manifest myself to you. I will be closer to you, where
you live now, in the twentieth century, than I was with
my disciples when I walked the hills of Galilee with
them!"

Because He Loved the Father

The chapter closes on a rather sinister note:

> *I will no longer talk much with you, for the
> ruler of this world is coming. He has no power
> over me; but I do as the Father has commanded
> me, so that the world may know that I love the
> Father. Rise, let us go hence.*   John 14:30, 31

Do you see the parallel he is drawing between what he
has just said to them and what he says of himself? He
says to us that if we love him we will obey him. If love is
in our hearts it will always issue in an obedient, trustful walk. And now he says that he goes toward the

bitterness and death of a cross. The ruler of this world is coming. He is going into an encounter with Satan— a bitter death-grapple in the darkness.

He did not have to go—*He has no power over me.* But he went because he loved the Father. Because he loved the Father he obeyed him. Ahead láy Gethsemane's agony, the cruel scourge, the mocking soldiers, the taunting of the Jews, the blood and the pain and the death and hell of the cross. What drove him to it? He went because he loved the Father and he wanted to give the Father his heart's desire. And what was that? *God so loved the world that he gave his only Son, that whoever believes in him should not perish but have eternal life* (John 3:16). That is what the Father wanted. And in order to give it to him, the Son obeyed him and went into the darkness and death of the cross.

When we must face into something we do not want to do, and our flesh cries out, "No! I don't want to go!" we can find the strength to do it by remembering who we are, to whom we belong, and that we will give our Lord the desire of his heart if we submit to what he has asked us to do.

Our heavenly Father, we pray that we may learn this great lesson, may learn to submit to your loving choices for us, and that we may drink the cup which you have given us to drink—for the Lord's sake, for his sake who loved us and gave himself for us. We ask in Jesus' name. Amen.

6

God's Vineyard
John 15:1-11

At the close of chapter 14 our Lord said to his disciples: *Rise, let us go hence.* So from this point on, we should no longer call this passage of Scripture the Upper Room Discourse. The remainder occurred as they were walking on their way to the Garden of Gethsemane. The traditional site of the Upper Room in Jerusalem is on the western side of the Old City, on the slopes of Mount Zion. You may have been there and seen it. If indeed this is the location, Jesus and his disciples would then have taken their way down across the Tyropoeon Valley, which separated the Temple from the rest of the city, around the wall skirting the Temple area, down into the Kidron Valley, across the brook, and then up the slope of the Mount of Olives to the Garden.

On the way they undoubtedly passed through the vineyards which surrounded the city. Jesus almost certainly must have stopped in the midst of a vineyard, taken a vine, and used it as a means of illustrating to his disciples the great secret he had been seeking to impart to them. This was the most fundamental and basic secret of Christian life—the secret which lay at the heart of his own experience and ministry: "I am in the Father, and the Father is in me"—and now the secret of their lives by the Spirit when he would come: "You in me, and I in you." He explained:

I am the true vine, and my Father is the vinedresser. Every branch of mine that bears no fruit, he takes away, and every branch that does bear fruit he prunes, that it may bear more fruit.
John 15:1, 2

72

His beautiful analogy has helped a great many Christians to understand the relationship God wants them to
know. In that unique way which was his, our Lord
took what lay at hand and made it unfold spiritual
truth.

When he said: *I am the true vine,* he did not mean
true in contrast with something false, fake, or counter-
feit, but rather real, genuine, as opposed to the mere
copy or symbol. As he held this vine and its branches
in his hand he indicated that this was the copy. *He*
was the true vine. He was the vine from which true life
is received.

And he included in that vine not only the branches,
but the stem and root. The whole plant was the vine.
By this he meant to illustrate the wonderful truth that
when we are united with Christ we are one with him,
we are identified with him. Later on, the Apostle Paul
would use another figure to bring out the same truth,
saying that every body has a head, and the body and
the head are one—they belong to each other (*see* Ephesians 4:15, 16). So the vine includes the branches, and
Jesus said, "I am that vine; you are the branches."

The purpose of this vine obviously, is to bring forth
fruit. A vineyard is planted not for ornamentation but
to produce grapes, to bear fruit. All through this account his emphasis was upon the fruit. So the question
arises at this point, "What does this fruit stand for in
our lives?" He is the vine, we are the branches. The
fruit is borne by the branches, produced by the vine.
What is that fruit?

Grapes of Joy

I am always amazed when people read this as though
the fruit were others won to Christ. How that can be
deduced from this parable is difficult to understand,
because nothing in it suggests that interpretation at
all. But many are troubled by those who claim that
unless a Christian is constantly winning others to
Christ he is a fruitless Christian. Let me reassure you
that this is not the case. Fruit, here, is that which is
produced by the vine and is the natural outflow of the
life of the vine. Although it is wonderful to have the
privilege of leading many to Christ, it is no indication

of fruitlessness if one has never had this experience.
The fruit here is not others won to Christ.

If we use the basic principle of understanding Scripture, which is common to all of Scripture—letting
Scripture interpret itself—there is no doubt as to what
this fruit is. The figure of the vine is used many times
in the Scriptures. These disciples, familiar with the
Old Testament, would immediately think of several
places where it was used. One is in Isaiah: *For the
vineyard of the Lord of hosts is the house* [the nation]
of Israel ... (Isaiah 5:7). And the psalmist said that
God brought a vine out of Egypt and planted it in a
good land (*see* Psalms 80:8). Israel was that vine.

As in Isaiah, God cleared out the rocks in his vineyard and hedged it about. He built a tower; he pro-
tected the vineyard and cared for it. He did everything
possible to cause it to produce grapes. But when he
came into his vineyard and looked for grapes, he found
wild grapes instead—sour, tastesless grapes. Isaiah
tells us what that represents:

> *For the vineyard of the Lord of hosts is the
> house of Israel, and the men of Judah are his
> pleasant planting; and he looked for justice, but
> behold, bloodshed; for righteousness, but be-
> hold, a cry!*   Isaiah 5:7

God came looking for justice and righteousness; instead he found oppression, cruelty, exploitation, and
indifference to the needs of others. So it is evident
from that parable that the fruit which God expects of
the vine is moral character, or as we have it in the
New Testament, the fruit of the Spirit—the fruit
which the Spirit produces. The life which is in the
vine produces fruit which Paul describes as: *love, joy,
peace, patience, kindness, goodness, faithfulness, gentleness, self-control* (*see* Galatians 5:22, 23). The fruit,
in other words, is Christlikeness. And our Lord indicates that the very purpose of the vine is to produce
such fruit.

The Father's Work

We Christians are God's great vineyard. The Father
is the vinedresser. He is responsible to see that the

purpose of the vine is fulfilled. And, as Jesus goes on to point out, he has a twofold work; first: *Every branch of mine that bears no fruit, he takes away....* That is, he cuts it off, he eliminates it from the life of the vine. We will see more of what that means as we go on in this account. Second: *and every branch that does bear fruit he prunes, that it may bear fruit.* He is teaching us here that right in the midst of the circumstances of life there can be more likeness to Christ, more of the moral character of Jesus—more fruit.

I struggled for a while with this word *prunes* because in the Greek it is really *cleanses*. It seemed to me that cleansing away debris was a far cry from pruning back the branches—until I learned that in the usual practice of viticulture (the care of vines), the branches are pruned back each year in order to cleanse them. A vine produces certain shoots (called sucker shoots) which start to grow where the branch joins the stem. If allowed to continue to grow, they would dissipate the life of the vine through so many branches that the vine would produce little or no fruit, but would produce leaves instead. So every vinedresser knows it is important to prune away these little sucker shoots in order that the vine may produce more fruit. And since they grow right where the branch joins the stem, creating a tight cluster where dirt, leaves, and other debris collect, the pruning is therefore a cleansing process. This is what our Lord had in view.

The Father's work is to find a branch which is beginning to bear fruit, beginning to produce the likeness of Christ, and to cut it back, trim off the shoots, so that it may bear more fruit. You can see what a beautiful analogy this is to the Christian experience, for in our lives we have that within us which produces the fruit of the Spirit. We do not have to work at it. We do not have to agonize and struggle to produce these qualities or characteristics; they are brought about naturally by the vine. Did you ever see a bunch of grapes struggling to hang onto the vine, trying to grow larger? No, it simply stays on the vine and lets the life of the vine produce the fruit.

Yet when this starts, the Father must trim back the branches. Our evil nature, our fallen Adamic nature,

produces in us those characteristics which are different from the fruit of the Spirit—resentment, anger,
bitterness, selfishness, egocentricity, love of praise—
qualities which tend to arise within us so frequently.
The Father is at work to cut them off, to prune them
back. What is the instrument he uses? Jesus tells us:

You are already made clean [pruned] *by the
word which I have spoken to you.*   John 15:3

Here in remarkable imagery he captures the work
which goes on in our lives as the Father employs the
circumstances in which we are found, the situations
of our lives, to make us heed and hear the Word which
corrects and changes. I am sure you have had the experience of being confronted with a portion of Scripture and learning from it that something you had been
doing all your life, and which you thought was right,
was actually wrong. Perhaps you were manifesting or
defending some attitude. Your whole family had done
it, and since it was a family characteristic, you thought
it was right. But you learned from the Word that it
was wrong. Perhaps for a while you paid no attention
to that Word (as many of us don't) and went on
blithely exhibiting this characteristic even though it
hurt you and hurt others—until the Father used some
circumstance to put you in such a place that you had to
listen to the Word. The hurt was too severe. You suddenly were confronted with what you were doing to
yourself and to others—you felt it and heard it and
saw it. That is the Father's pruning knife cutting off
the sucker shoots of the old life within us, so that we
might produce more of the Christlikeness, the fruit of
the Spirit. This is the work of the Father.

He not only does this, but he does it repeatedly. Notice that Jesus says here to the disciples: *You are
already made clean.* That is, "This pruning has gone
on in your life already." But that was not the end of
it; there was to be more as they went on. In a vineyard the vines are pruned not just once in their life-
times; the process is repeated every spring. There is
a pruning time, a pruning season.

Are you going through a pruning season right now?

Is God using the sharp knife of circumstances to cut off the sucker shoot of an old habit or attitude in your life, confronting you with that word of truth which corrects and cleanses, causing you to see it and feel it and hear it and give heed to it? Well, that is the work of the Father, and it is done in order that you might bear more fruit, be more like Jesus in your reactions—in your home, in your shop, in your recreation, wherever you may be with people—that you may be like Christ.

Now our Lord goes on to set forth, in the most helpful way I know of in all of Scripture, what might be called the Law of Fruitfulness: *Abide in me, and I in you.* There he is, back on the subject of that basic relationship which is already established by the coming of the Holy Spirit into an individual's life: "You in me, and I in you." But now he adds this note of responsibility—there is something which *you* must do. The relationship is not merely to be recognized; it is to be acted upon:

> *Abide in me, and I in you. As the branch cannot bear fruit by itself, unless it abides in the vine, neither can you, unless you abide in me. I am the vine, you are the branches. He who abides in me, and I in him, he it is that bears much fruit, for apart from me you can do nothing.*
>
> John 15:4, 5

This is an extremely helpful passage! Notice that our Lord divides it into two sections. There is an activity which is to be done, and a passivity which is to be acknowledged—an active voice and a passive voice. We are to abide in him (that is active, something we do), and we are to let him abide in us (that is passive, something we allow him to do). Both these relationships are absolutely essential, not one as opposed to the other, but both together.

Choose to Maintain the Relationship

When our Lord says: *Abide in me* he is talking about the will, about the choices, the decisions we make. We must decide to do things which expose ourselves to him and keep ourselves in contact with him. This is what it means to abide in him. We have been placed into Christ by the Holy Spirit. Now we must choose to maintain that relationship by the decisions we make—decisions to expose ourselves to his Word in order to learn about him, and to relate to him in prayer wherein we converse with him. Decisions to relate to other believers in Body Life experiences; that is, bearing one another's burdens and confessing our faults and sharing in fellowship with one another, wherein we learn about and see Christ in one another. All of this is designed to relate to him—*Abide in me.* If we do that, we are fulfilling this active, necessary decision of the will to obey his Word, to do what he says, and to stay in touch with him.

This is what Bible study and prayer are all about. They are not mere mechanical practices which every Christian ought to do in order to stay "in" with the crowd, or to maintain his "membership card," or to get "brownie points" with God. No, they are means through which we can know him. If you open your Bible and begin to read it without the conscious expectation that it is going to tell you something about him, you will read in vain. If you try to pray as though it were some exercise in which you chalk off fifteen minutes' worth, mechanically going through a list like the turning of a prayer wheel, it is a valueless experience.

But if you pray because you are talking with One whom you love and want to know more of, sharing with him out of the fullness of your heart, then prayer becomes a beautiful and marvelous experience. One of the delights of life is to spend time in that kind of prayer. If, in relating to others you merely get together and have coffee and talk about the weather, you will find it useless. But if you share where you are spiritually, what your struggles are, what you are going through, and if you bear one another's burdens and love each other in the Lord, it becomes a delightful, marvelous, strengthening experience. Christ then becomes real to you. That is abiding in him.

Decide—And Rest

But that is only part of it. Jesus says, "Abide in me, *and I in you.*" There is also the other side—"Let me abide in you." What does that mean? Well, that has to do with empowerment, enablement. You see, you can make choices but you cannot fulfill them. And although you are responsible to make the decisions and make the choices, you are not responsible for the power to carry them out. There you are to depend on him, to let him abide in you. You are to rest upon his ability to see you through, to work it out. As you venture out on that basis you expect him to support you and to carry you through.

Both of these are absolutely essential, and our Lord develops this fact. He says, first: *As the branch cannot bear fruit by itself, unless it abides in the vine, neither can you, unless you abide in me.* That is, "If you do not abide in me, you will be fruitless." If you will not make the decisions that expose you to his truth and love, you will most certainly produce a fruitless Christian life—faith without works, which is dead. But, he says: *He who abides in me, and I in him, he it is that bears much fruit, for apart from me you can do nothing.* That is, if you try to make all the choices and carry all the responsibility yourself, you will also lead a fruitless life. If you depend upon your determination or your will power to live the Christian life, you will find that it is mechanical and dead. *Without me you can do nothing.*

Both of these are necessary in the Christian experience. We must make choices, we must determine to expose ourselves to him, we must seek his face in the Word and in prayer and in fellowship with others. And then we must rest on him, count on him to see us through, to supply that enabling power which makes us able to love and forgive and rejoice and give thanks, even when everything is going wrong. When we do, we are abiding in him and letting him abide in us. Without *both* of these, fruitlessness is the result.

You see, you can do many things without depending on Christ. He does not mean that without him you remain just an immobile blob. You can operate your business without Christ. You can make it run well.

You can raise your family without Christ. You can even pastor a church without Christ. But if you do, you will find that there will be no fruit, no Christlikeness, no manifestation of that beautiful character which arrests the attention of others. Instead there will be a sham, a phony imitation of the real thing, which will drive people away from Christ and will produce nothing but a dull, mechanical religiosity which is piousness without God.

Our Lord goes on now to point out the consequence of not abiding in him:

> *If a man does not abide in me, he is cast forth as a branch and withers; and the branches are gathered, thrown into the fire and burned.*
>
>   John 15:6

Here is the case of our Lord mentioned earlier when he said, of one aspect of the Father's work: *Every branch of mine that bears no fruit, he takes away.* Here is the process in which the branch is cut off, and then it withers—grows dry and dull and dead. Many churchgoers are in that state. They may have been members of churches for years, but there is no life evident at all. Eventually these branches are to be gathered and burned. I believe this is a reference to other passages in Scripture which say that the angels will be sent out to gather up all that offends in God's Kingdom and cast it into the eternal fire where it will be burned (*see* Matthew 13:40-42).

Judas was a paramount example of this. He was with the Lord—spent three and a half years with him. He even shared in the experience of ministry with the other disciples. He exercised the power of God by performing miracles. But there was no life in him. He did not abide in Christ, and Christ did not abide in him. As a result he was cut off, and he withered. The withering process was very short in his case. He committed suicide within a few days, and he was burned—eternally lost. This is a picture of those church members who, despite attending church, never have any manifestation of truth, never have any sign in their lives of that quality of love and forgiveness and understand-

ing and compassion which is born of the Holy Spirit,
but are rigid and narrow and hard and harsh and con-
demning and difficult—even though they say and do
the "right" thing.

On the other hand, our Lord gives us the results of
fruit-bearing—four beautiful manifestations. First:

> *If you abide in me, and my words abide in you*
> [this is the way we let him abide in us—by his
> Word], *ask whatever you will, and it shall be*
> *done for you.*   John 15:7

Answered prayer is one of the first signs of a fruitful
life. It is not part of the fruit itself; it is the result of
a life which is becoming increasingly Christlike. The
result will be, "Ask what you will. . . ." St. Augustine
once gathered up this very truth in a beautiful way:
"Love God, and do as you please." That frightens some
people. All they hear is, "Do as you please." But it
must be preceded by that vital phrase, "Love God."
When you love God, then all that you do is touched and
controlled by love, and love is the fulfilling of the Law.
So you can do what you please when you love God. And
if you truly love him, you can ask whatever you will.
This is the glory of Christian liberty. Prayers are
answered, growing out of that relationship of an obedient and dependent heart—leaving the process and
timing to God. You cannot tell him *when* to answer
your prayers. You cannot tell him *how* to answer your
prayers. But he *will answer* your prayers when they
grow out of this relationship.

Do You Want to Be Recognized?

Second, there is the demonstration of discipleship:

> *By this my Father is glorified, that you bear*
> *much fruit, and so prove to be my disciples.*
>   John 15:8

God is glorified when his people bear fruit and manifest Christlikeness. You don't even have to do a thing
to manifest his character. You can be flat on your back
in bed, sick, but manifesting a Christlike spirit, and

you are glorifying God by that experience. It is not
activity which glorifies God, it is character; it is what
you are, and the way you react to a situation. Do you
want to be known as a disciple of Jesus? Do you want
to be recognized as one who follows Jesus? Well then,
abide in him, and he in you. That is the way that your
discipleship is manifested.

A friend of mine operates a very unusual ranch. It
is designed as a guest ranch for affluent people. The
man who owns it has a heart of concern for what he
calls the "up-and-outers," those who are overprivi-
leged, who have too much of everything, yet to whom
very few are witnessing, telling them of life in Christ.
So he has designed this ranch for that purpose. People
come and spend a lot of money, staying a week or so at
a time. There are no Bible studies, no meetings; it is a
very low-key approach.

What the owner does is to go throughout the country interviewing young people for the crew to work on
this ranch. He will interview perhaps three hundred
young people and from them select maybe thirty. He
asks them only three questions. First: "Do you love
work?", because they are going to have to work from
seven in the morning until sometimes ten or eleven at
night. Then: "Do you love people; do you like to be
with people and relate to them?" They must satisfy
him that they love people. The third question is: "Do
you love Jesus?" If they can assure him that they love
work, love people, and love Jesus, then they have a
tremendous opportunity to work at that ranch.

When the guests arrive, the crew simply relates to
them and gives them the time of their lives. By the
third evening the guests are all asking, "Where did
you ever get this tremendous crew of young people?
What a fantastic group they are!" And that evening,
the owner of the ranch sits down and says, "Many of
you have been asking about our crew. Let me tell you
why they are the way they are." And he tells them
about the three questions he asked: Do you love work?;
Do you love people?; Do you love Jesus? He says,
"Now, it may seem strange to you that I should ask
that last question. But I have learned that the only
young people who can ever meet this grueling demand

with an unvarying spirit of joy and gladness, with the kind of attitude that has so impressed you, are those who have learned to love Jesus."

From then on there are still no meetings, but invariably there are those guests who come and say, "I want to know more about this." And there is conversion after conversion throughout the remainder of the week—because of young people who manifest by their lives that they are Jesus' disciples. They *prove* to be his disciples.

An Overflowing Cup

The third result is the deeper experience of Christ's love:

> *As the Father has loved me, so have I loved you; abide in my love. If you keep my commandments, you will abide in my love, just as I have kept my Father's commandments and abide in his love.*   John 15:9, 10

Remember that earlier in the passage our Lord had said, "If you love me, you will keep my commandments." And from that we saw that obedience grows out of love of Jesus for us, shed abroad in our hearts by the Holy Spirit, which awakens our love toward him in reponse. When our hearts are moved by love it is easy to obey his Word, for we obey the One we love. He adds here the ingredient that when we obey his Word, keep his commandments, we will *abide* in his love. We will have a continuing sense and experience of his love for us. So it is a complete cycle which keeps producing deeper and deeper experiences of love.

All of us have learned, one way or another, that love demands a response if it is to grow. If you love somebody, and reach out toward him, you can go only so far unless he responds to that love. If he responds just a little, then your love can reach out further, can deepen and grow. But if he remains unresponsive over the weeks and months and years, love finally is limited to that initial step of reaching out. But where love has a response, it grows deeper and richer and truer, and eventually becomes a glorious experience. If you are not feeling the depth of love you would like to experience, one of the reasons may be that you are not responding to the love which is already reaching out to you. That is why the New Testament says, "Open your hearts, widen your hearts, be responsive—love back." When you do that, then love grows into this deepening, quickening experience.

Then the last result of fruit-bearing—the fullness of joy:

> *These things I have spoken to you, that my joy may be in you, and that your joy may be full.*
> **John 15:11**

His joy, the joy that was always there at the bottom of his heart, that gladness of relationship with his Father, is now to be our experience. Joy, that sense of gladness of relationship with him, will increase as we go. I love the saying: Joy is the flag which flies over the castle of the heart when the King is in residence. That is what joy is—this sense of our unity with Jesus, the sense of his power, his adequacy, his ability to handle the problems which are thrust upon us. Let all that be present in the heart, and the face will light up with joy!

That is what Jesus is talking about. *Abide in me, and I in you,* and you will be fruitful—without realizing it, manifesting the characteristics of the Spirit, the fruit of the Spirit, the quality of life which is like Jesus. When that happens, there will come these additional benefits: answered prayer, a glorifying of the Father through the demonstration of discipleship, a deepening of the experience of love, and joy made full. What a wonderful relationship our Lord taught us here by this lesson of the vine!

Our Father, as you walk through your vineyard, looking at the various vines, you see sucker shoots on some which need to be pruned away. Thank you for your faithfulness in being at work to do that. On others you see luscious, tempting, delicious fruit which gladdens and delights your heart, glorifies you, and we thank you for that. We know that your work with us is to the end that we may produce more fruit, that this vineyard will be such a fruitful place as to make the world around us yearn to know the secret of such fruit. We thank you for these possibilities which we have in Jesus Christ our Lord. We pray in his name. Amen.

Love and Hate
John 15:12—16:4

All of us are concerned about priorities—about what comes first, and what to do next. Jesus now sets forth, in order, the fundamental priorities of life.

Above all else, as we have seen in the first eleven verses of chapter 15, the Christian's relationship to the Lord is of supreme importance. If this area is hurting in your life, stop everything else you are doing and get it straightened out! If you go on in that condition you will hurt not only yourself but others as well. It is so important that you maintain this relationship, which our Lord puts in the simple words: *Abide in me, and I in you.*

The second and third priorities of life are found in the remainder of the chapter and the first four verses of chapter 16. The second is our relationship to other believers, expressed in the words: *Love one another.* The third is the relationship we have to the world outside—a world which hates and persecutes, and yet toward which the attitude of the Christian is to be, we shall see, one of patient witness.

Love Is Not an Option

Regarding our relationship to other believers Jesus says:

This is my commandment, that you love one another as I have loved you. Greater love has no man than this, that a man lay down his life for his friends. You are my friends if you do what I command you. No longer do I call you servants, for the servant does not know what his master is doing; but I have called you friends, for all that I have heard from my Father I have

*made known to you. You did not choose me, but
I chose you and appointed you that you should
go and bear fruit and that your fruit should
abide; so that whatever you ask the Father in
my name, he may give it to you. This I command
you, to love one another.*   John 15:12-17

Notice that this paragraph begins and ends with the
command of Jesus, "I command you to love one another." The fact that this is put in the imperative
mode means it is not an option in our life. It is not
something we do if we feel like it. It is not to be an
occasional action on our part. It is to be a deliberate
response to another person whom we know to be in the
family of God, regardless of how we feel toward that
person.

Many people struggle at this point. They say, "How
can you command love? Love is a feeling; how can
anyone command me to love someone I don't love, or
to stop loving someone I do? Love is our master; we do
not master it." Those who speak in this way reveal a
very serious misconception of love. They are unfortunately victims of Hollywood in this respect. They
think of love as a feeling of affection toward another
—sometimes a very sentimental, romantic feeling.

But love, as Jesus speaks of it here, is far different.
We can be sure of one thing: he would never command
us to do what is impossible for us to do. The secret,
of course, is that we are to love, he says: . . . *as I have
loved you.* This kind of love is to arise out of the same
kind of relationship that he had with the Father and
that made it possible for him to love us. In this same
manner, and from the same source, we are to love one
another with the same quality of love. He loved us
because God is love, and he was indwelt by the Father.
He was in the Father, and the Father in him. *As he
yielded to that relationship, love flowed out.* It could
not help it—God is love. We are to love one another
because we are in the Son, and the Son in us. Since
God is love, as we yield to that relationship to the Son,
love flows from us. And it will have the qualities that
his love had.

He goes on to define for us three aspects of love

88   SECRETS OF THE SPIRIT

which mark the quality of his love for us, and which we also are to show to one another. The first is given in the words: *Greater love has no man than this, that a man lay down his life for his friends.* Love lays down its life for another. We all know how fully Jesus himself exemplified this. He laid down his life for us. This, he says, is the greatest love that anyone can demonstrate toward his friends. Some have said, "Wouldn't it be a greater love to love your enemies?" In his Letter to the Romans, Paul tells us that God's love was of such quality that he loved us even when we were enemies (*see* Romans 5:10). It is true, that is a greater kind of love. But here our Lord is talking about what you can do for your *friends.* You can show no greater love for your friends than to lay down your life for them.

Time for Your Friends

Obviously this means more than simply dying physically for them. If it meant only that, there would be very few of us who could or would ever fulfill this, largely because we would lack the opportunity to do so. Besides, one could do so only once! But our Lord is commanding us to do this repeatedly. So he means by this that we are to give ourselves up for one another. That is what laying down our life means—giving something of ourselves to another. When you go out of your way to meet a friend's need, when you are willing to spend time with someone who is a Christian just because he is a Christian, not necessarily because you are drawn to him, you are laying down your life, a part of it at least, for that person. This is what Jesus has in mind.

One of the interns at our church made a study on the words *one another* in the New Testament. It gathered up, both negatively and positively, all the teaching of the New Testament on relationship one to another in the family of God. Negatively the New Testament says:

Don't challenge one another.
Don't complain against one another.
Don't devour one another.

Don't envy one another.
Don't judge one another.
Don't lie to one another.
Don't speak against one another.

And positively it says:

Accept one another.
Admonish one another.
Bear one another's burdens.
Bear up one another.
Bear with one another.
Care for one another.
Comfort one another.
Confess your sins to one another.
Encourage one another.
Fellowship with one another.
Forgive one another.
Greet one another.
Honor one another.
Be hospitable toward each other.
Humble yourself toward one another.
Be kind to one another.
Love one another.
Be members one of another.
Pray for one another.
Be at peace with one another.
Have the same mind toward one another.
Seek after that which is good for one another.
Serve one another.
Show forebearance to one another.
Stimulate one another.
Be subject to one another.
Teach one another.
Be tenderhearted one toward another.

What a full range of relationships our Lord has caught up in this command that we are to love one another, even to the extent of laying down our lives—giving up our own comforts—for one another!

The Mark of Friendship

The second mark of his kind of love is that it shares its secrets:

*No longer do I call you servants, for the servant
does not know what his master is doing; but I
have called you friends, for all that I have heard
from my Father I have made known to you.*
                                                            John 15:15

This is a remarkable statement. In the sense that he
shares with them his life and the secrets of his inner-
most heart, they have become his friends. Now, this is
not the only relationship which believers have with
the Lord. They remain his servants, and a little later
he refers to them as such: *A servant is not greater
than his master* (John 15:20). But in this sense, we
are friends of Jesus.

What do you do with a friend? The first mark of
friendship is sharing. You tell him secrets and share
opportunities with him. If you get a hot tip on the
stock market you call up your friend—so he can buy
first and see if it's any good! If you run into a bar-
gain at a department store you share the news with a
friend. If you have an opportunity to enjoy some unusual experience you call up your friend. Friendship
is always marked by the sharing of intimacy.

Our Lord says that he has shared the secrets of his
life with his disciples—and with us. He tells them
what the Father has told him about life, about death,
about hell, about heaven, about relationships one with
another, about history, about the world. He pours it
all out, tells them what he has known, what he has
learned from the Father. This is the mark and characteristic of love.

In other words, he is talking about what we at our
church have learned to call *Body Life*. We are to love
one another in the same way Jesus loved us. As he told
his disciples what he had learned, so we are to share
with one another what we have learned—our struggles,
our fears, our hopes, our experiences, all that God has
taught us by what we have gone through. If the church
is nothing more than a crowd of people coming together and listening to a speaker, then it is no different from a convention or a conference on some secular
theme. What makes it different is that we share our

lives with one another. There is the unfolding of secrets, the bearing of burdens, telling of one another's
needs, touching of one another's lives. This is what it
means to love one another. Some time ago I culled this
from a church bulletin:

You ever feel like a frog? Frogs feel slow, low, ugly, puffy,
drooped, pooped. I know—one told me. The frog feeling
comes when you want to be bright but feel dumb, when you
want to share but are selfish, when you want to be thankful
but feel resentment, when you want to be great but are
small, when you want to care but are indifferent. Yes, at one
time or another each of us has found himself on a lily pad,
floating down the great river of life. Frightened and dis-
gusted, we're too froggish to budge.

Once upon a time there was a frog, only he really wasn't
a frog—he was a prince who looked and felt like a frog. A
wicked witch had cast a spell on him. Only the kiss of a
beautiful maiden could save him. But since when do cute
chicks kiss frogs? So there he sat, unkissed prince in frog
form. But miracles happen. One day a beautiful maiden
gathered him up and gave him a great big smack. Crash!
Boom! Zap! There he was, a handsome prince. And you
know the rest—they lived happily ever after.

So what is the task of the church? Kissing frogs, of
course!

That is what Jesus is saying to us, isn't it? *Love one
another.*

Compassion Fruit

The last element of this love is defined as the bearing of fruit in one another's lives through prayer:

*You did not choose me, but I chose you and ap-
pointed you that you should go and bear fruit
and that your fruit should abide; so that whatever you ask the Father in my name, he may
give it to you.*   John 15:16

As you put this all together you see that the mark of
love he is talking about here is the bearing of fruit by
means of prayer. The context is still the example of
love which he set. This is what he did—he prayed for
his own. He will pray for them again, as recorded in

chapter 17, and thus bear fruit in their lives. The fruit in view here is, as we have seen all along, Christlikeness. It is the character of Jesus, the compassion, the gentleness, the forgiving quality, the courage, the strength, the beauty, the grace of his life. This is what we are to bear, not only in our own lives but in one another's lives, by means of prayer. As we pray for one another we help each other bear the fruit of Christlikeness.

This is why the Epistles remind us to pray for all saints, to make supplication for one another, to pray for one another. This is the means by which we love one another. And this is our Lord's command. We are not to treat each other with disdain but we are to reach out in this way toward one another. At a Christian gathering recently I heard someone speaking of another, say, "I can't stand that person, and I don't want anything to do with her!" That is a violation of our Lord's command to love one another.

Love means to give yourself for another, to give of your life and strength and time for another. Love means to share with and teach one another what you have learned. And love means to pray for one another. John tells us that if any man says, "I love God," but hates his brother, he is a liar (*see* 1 John 4:20). If we love God we are also to love one another. This is the great command which makes the difference between the church, as a community of those who love each other, and the world around us, which essentially neglects and is indifferent to one another. This is also what makes the Christian witness, as we will see a little later.

In the next section our Lord goes on to point out the priority and some elements of the relationship of the Christian to the world around him. He begins with the attitude of the world toward the Christian:

If the world hates you, know that it has hated me before it hated you. If you were of the world, the world would love its own; but because you are not of the world, but I chose you out of the world, therefore the world hates you.
                                                              John 15:18, 19

It is remarkable that our Lord moves so quickly from his words about love for one another to this word about the hatred of the world toward the Christian. The world, as our Lord is using the term, refers to secular society, *not* humanity. Humanity does not hate the church; it is the *world* which hates the church— and the Lord of the church. The world is organized society, without God, but with its own morals and standards and value systems. It is what we ordinarily call "the system," and *it* is what hates the believer and wants nothing to do with him.

The world, as our Lord says, both hates and loves. It loves what conforms to it; it hates what differs with it. We have all experienced this. We know that even in small, nonreligious matters the world can hate anything which does not conform to it. I read the other day that the man who invented the umbrella was pelted with rotten eggs and vegetables and stones when he first tried it out on a public street. No one else had one, you see. So the world loves to destroy that which does not fit its pattern.

This is why the Scriptures urge us to not be conformed to the world around us: "Do not let the world squeeze you into its own mold" (*see* Romans 12:2)— for it desperately dislikes anything which differs with it, and will try to change it. If we do conform to the world, if the church is worldly—not so much in terms of its actions, but in having certain attitudes—if the church trusts in its own power and seeks for prestige and status, and acts as though God does not add anything to it—then the world loves the church. It will pat it on the back and praise it and exalt it. But it hates and stands against any church which is true to its Lord.

Twentieth-Century Persecution

Our Lord points out that the world will not only hate, but it will also persecute the church:

> *Remember the word that I said to you, "A servant is not greater than his master." If they persecuted me, they will persecute you; if they kept my word, they will keep your also.*
> John 15:20

Not only does the world hate the believer, but it also
moves actively to get rid of Christian faith, Christian
teaching, and even Christians. This has been demon-
strated all through history. It may surprise you to
know that, in all the twenty centuries since our Lord
was here, the century which has seen more outright,
vicious, violent persecution of Christians is not the
first but the twentieth. More Christians are being
hated and destroyed, their goods and homes confiscated,
their persons attacked and mistreated in this century
than in any other. I think immediately of those in
Russia and other communist countries. Communism
always hates Christianity, and those who stand for it
and are committed teachers of it are always first on
the list for destruction whenever a communist government takes over.

Nevertheless, Jesus says, some will receive: *If they
kept my word, they will keep yours also*. This is the
encouragement to the witness of the church—that not
all will hate, not all will persecute. Some will receive,
some will believe, some will give heed and respond, as
they did with Jesus. From these words we can understand that the church need never expect to win the
masses of people to Christ. Jesus didn't. Even the tremendous witness he gave to the nation in his day did
not win the majority to himself. The witness of the
church will have the same effect.

As our Lord continues, he gives us the reasons for
the world's attitude:

*But all this they will do to you on my account,
because they do not know him who sent me.*
                                    John 15:21

The first reason for the attitude of hatred and persecution is that of ignorance. The world does not know
God. It does not understand him. It has a distorted
and twisted view of him. It thinks of him as an arbi-
trary ruler, a great judge or policeman—if it thinks
of him at all. It does not know his compassion, his
forgiveness, his tenderness, his patience, his willing-
ness to work with the slightest response. So the world,

in ignorance, persecutes God. Jesus describes this very ignorance:

> *They will put you out of the synagogues; indeed, the hour is coming when whoever kills you will think he is offering service to God.* John 16:2

That is how blind they are. They actually think they are worshiping God, for that is what the words *offering service* mean. They think they are worshiping God by persecuting and killing Christians. This was true during the early days of Christian persecution, again during the days of the Inquisition, and it is still true today in many ways and forms. Of course, there is no greater example that Saul of Tarsus, that brilliant Young Pharisee who was burning with threats and hatred in his heart toward the early Christians. In persecuting them he thought he was actually serving God, pleasing God in this way. Later on when he became Paul the Apostle he tells us: ... *I received mercy because I had acted ignorantly in unbelief* (1 Timothy 1:13).

We Christians need constantly to bear in mind how ignorant the world is. It does not know truth, although it thinks it does. It talks as though it knew great and startling truth. But when it comes right down to a confrontation with the truth as it is in Jesus, the world is abysmally ignorant. That is one reason it persecutes believers.

Men Still Love Darkness

But there is a second reason, and Jesus goes on to point out that deliberate rejection persists, even when ignorance has been corrected:

> *If I had not come and spoken to them, they would not have sin; but now they have no excuse for their sin. He who hates me hates my Father also. If I had not done among them the works which no one else did, they would not have sin; but now they have seen and hated both me and my Father. It is to fulfil the word that is written in their law, "They hated me without cause."*
> John 15:22-25

Now ignorance has been met; the light has come. As John says in the early part of his Gospel: *And this is the judgment, that the light has come into the world, and men* [still] *loved darkness rather than light, because their deeds were evil* (John 3:19). Knowing the truth, they rejected it.

This is further evidence of the enmity of the world. Jesus came and spoke words of truth; he came and did deeds of love. What he said revealed the way things really are, took away the veils and illusions, and revealed truth and reality. What he did revealed the love of the Father, the kindness, the compassion, the healing ability, the qualities of God. But as people saw his works and heard his words, they rejected them and this resulted in increasing hatred and violence, culminating at last in the Crucifixion, in their nailing him to a cross. And, as he said, there was no excuse—they hated him without a cause.

What, then, is to be the attitude of the Christian to this kind of world in which we still live? Our Lord's answer follows:

But when the Counselor [the Comforter, the Strengthener] *comes, whom I shall send to you from the Father, even the Spirit of truth, who proceeds from the Father, he will bear witness to me; and you also are witnesses, because you have been with me from the beginning.*
                                                    John 15:26, 27

Obviously the primary reference here is to the apostles themselves, for they *were* with him from the beginning. But it also applies to us. He says, "When the Spirit of God has come, you will bear witness of me to this world." The world is not to be left in its hopeless rejection of Christ—even though it has resisted and rejected truth when it knew it to be truth. We have all been part of this, haven't we? Every one of us has done this. Still, God does not abandon us. Isn't that amazing? Even when he would be fully justified in turning his back and walking away and leaving us all to our own consequences, he does not do so. He continues to bear a witness before the world.

So the Christian is not to retaliate, not to resent the hatred and persecution of the world, not to be vindictive, nor return evil for evil. Rather, we are exhorted to return good for evil. Nor are we to retire from the world, to withdraw from it and build a Christian ghetto in which to hide ourselves, and then to throw tracts across the chasm! Rather, we are to move into the world, live in its midst just as Jesus did, and bear witness to the truth even though it is often rejected. We are to do this for the sake of those who *will* receive, who will believe, will accept the Word. We are to bear witness in the midst of the world.

This witness is twofold. Primarily it is the witness of the Holy Spirit, who does what no man can do. The Spirit of God prepares hearts, removes blindness, opens minds to understand. He bears witness that a word is true, gives it a ring of authenticity; therefore, power in witnessing rests with the Spirit, not with us. But we are to bear witness too. As Jesus indicates here, we are to bear witness as the apostles did—as to what they saw and heard, what they themselves experienced. Just before his Ascension Jesus said: *But you shall receive power when the Holy Spirit has come upon you; and you shall be my witnesses* ... (Acts 1:8). We are all to be witnesses of what Jesus has been to us, what we have experienced, what has happened in our lives, what he has done for us. And the Holy Spirit will witness with that, using those words, simple as they may be, to open minds and to break through hard hearts, to pierce and break down barriers, and to open people up to the World. Thus the business of the church is to witness before a hating world.

Fiery Ordeals? Of Course!

Our Lord closes this section with his reason for teaching along this line:

I have said all this to you to keep you from falling away. They will put you out of the synagogues; indeed, the hour is coming when whoever kills you will think he is offering service to

*God. And they will do this because they have not
known the Father, nor me. But I have said these
things to you, that when their hour comes you
may remember that I told you of them.*

John 16:1–4

He does not want his disciples to be taken by surprise.
If we run into mistreatment, if our witness is rejected,
if we are persecuted or hated or ostracized, or treated
with disdain or scorn by the world, we are to understand that this was predicted. It is part of the course,
a natural event. Remember what Peter tells us: *Beloved, do not be surprised at the fiery ordeal which
comes upon you to prove you, as though something
strange were happening to you* (1 Peter 4:12). It is
not strange, it is part of the process. *And man's foes
will be those of his own household* (Matthew 10:36).
They will be your enemies, they will bear false witness against you. They will turn against you, sometimes when you least expect it.

"But," Jesus says, "do not be surprised. This is the
enmity we are to expect, the warfare in which we are
engaged. Do not be surprised, but remember that I
told you in advance because you are my friends, and I
keep no secrets from you." He brings us again to the
remembrance of the intimacy of the relationship we
have with him, and of the fact that we are to witness
on the basis of the power which we are provided by
abiding in him, and are to support that witness by
having a spirit of loving acceptance toward one another which tenderly cares for one another, shares with
one another, prays for one another. Thus the world is
confronted with a testimony it cannot gainsay, a character it cannot deny, which will either turn men in
bitterness against God, or draw them by the Spirit to
him. This is the work of the church today. May God
help us as we seek to fulfill it in this twentieth-century
hour!

Father, how many times have we sung the words, "Faith of our fathers, holy faith; we will be true to thee till death." Lord, we pray that you will keep us in the midst of this unbelieving, rejecting world, and will help us to rejoice as we have the privilege of bearing witness to a crucified Saviour. Let us do, Lord, as Jesus himself told us to do: "Rejoice and give thanks when men revile you and persecute you and say all manner of evil against you falsely for my sake." Lord, we ask that you will strengthen us and help us to reach out in love, one toward another, and to the weary world around us in their blindness and ignorance, so that we may bear witness of Jesus Christ, our true and loving Lord. We ask in his name. Amen.

8

The Message of the Spirit
John 16:4–15

As our Lord spoke to his disciples in the Upper Room and on the way to the Garden, there were two great themes which occupied his heart. The first was to reveal to them the secret of his own life, the great principle which enabled him to function as he did, to act in the unforgettable way which was his. The secret, he said, was his relationship to the Father. The Father was in him, and he was in the Father. The second great theme he was seeking to impress upon these disciples was the relationship they would need in order to handle life after he had left them. It would be the coming Holy Spirit who would make available to them the same principle of life by which he himself had lived. Then it would be the Son in them, and they in him. This was to be the secret of their life. So, much of this passage deals with the ministry and message of the Holy Spirit.

After our Lord has revealed the hostility of the world which the disciples would face after he left them —the persecution and judgment and death—he now says to them:

I did not say these things to you from the beginning, because I was with you. But now I am going to him who sent me; yet none of you asks me, "Where are you going?" But because I have said these things to you, sorrow has filled your hearts. Nevertheless I tell you the truth: it is to your advantage that I go away, for if I do not go away, the Counselor will not come to you; but if I go, I will send him to you.

John 16:4–7

100

This passage opens with an explanation of the need of man for the Spirit of God. It is revealed to us in the condition of these disciples. Our Lord has indicated to them that there were certain things he did not say to them from the beginning. He did not tell them of the hostility of the world. He did not tell them about the tremendous opposition and persecution they would face. Nor did he tell them how to meet it. And he says why: *I did not say these things to you from the beginning, because I was with you.* There he indicates our need as human beings to be kept and supported and strengthened. He was keeping these disciples himself. Since he was there, they had no need to know all that he was keeping them from, or how it was done. "But now," he says, "I'm going away. Now you'll need to understand what has been happening."

There he reveals to us the basic need of our humanity: to be kept. This is what the Scriptures teach us about ourselves—that we are basically born to be dependent on something or someone else. We are not able to handle life by ourselves. No one is. The Big Lie, which has been circulated since the fall of man, is that man is independent, that he does not need anything, that he can be self-sufficient. He can run his own life, make his own decisions, and handle everything himself. How widespread that notion is! You see it reflected everywhere—especially among youth, who are confident that they know how to handle life. Nothing is going to trap them, or trick them, or deceive them. How delusive that is! Our Lord indicates here that these disciples had been able to exist only because he was with them and kept them.

The Strengthener

Now, as he leaves, they are occupied not with what he has told them, but with themselves. Because Jesus says: *I am going to him who sent me; yet none of you asks me, "Where are you going?"*, it is evident that our Lord expects these men to question him. He is attempting to arouse their curiosity. He is saying to them, "Why don't you ask me some questions? Aren't you interested in what is going to happen, what the result of

my going away is going to be?" Instead, all they can
think of is what it might mean to them. They are occupied with themselves, just as we are, and can see
only their own little world. And so, as he says: *Sorrow
has filled your hearts.* Instead of curiosity, and the
consequent knowledge they could have, and even an
excitement about what is going to happen, sorrow has
filled their hearts and they are occupied with themselves. What a revelation of what we are! We need
someone to keep us. That Someone who keeps us today
is the Holy Spirit, as our Lord goes on to say:

> *Nevertheless I tell you the truth: it is to your
> advantage that I go away, for if I do not go
> away, the Counselor will not come to you; but
> if I go, I will send him to you.*   John 16:7

I am sure that you have often felt, as I have, that these
disciples had a great advantage over us. To sit and
listen to Jesus, to hear his words, to see his face, to
see how he acted, to be with him in the midst of his
miracles, to walk with him and listen to him and watch
him—what an advantage they had! How many of us
have felt, "Oh, if only we could have been there, if
only we could have seen what these disciples saw!"
Yet Jesus is telling them very frankly, "Look, it is
going to be better for you when I leave. It will be
better for you when I go away, for when I go away
the Strengthener will come." I like that translation of
the word. It is the Strengthener, the One who meets
our needs from within, who is coming to us. That is
what these disciples needed, and what we need.

I know it is hard for us to believe that it would be
better for Jesus' disciples when he had gone. But have
you noticed in reading through the Gospels that when
Jesus finished the Sermon on the Mount, or even this
Upper Room Discourse, or any of his great messages,
that the disciples ever went away with their faces
aglow, their minds understanding, their hearts committed, and ready to work? No, the record tells us
instead that every time he talked to them he puzzled
them. They were perplexed, they couldn't figure him
out, and they went away arguing about what he had

to say. They were full of questions, and they disputed among themselves as to who was going to fulfill these things, vying with each other for first place.

But after the day of Pentecost, when the Spirit came, when they gathered together and heard the words of the Lord, they went away tremendously strengthened and encouraged, ready to face life with radiant faces and joy in their hearts. That is what the Spirit does. It was indeed to their advantage, and to ours, that Jesus was not with them. Suppose he were here in the world today, right now. Where would he be? Well, probably somewhere else than where you are. And how would you ever get to see him? Yet, by means of the Spirit we have access to him, as these disciples never had.

Who Receives the Spirit?

Now our Lord goes on to point out the ministry of the Spirit, the way he would work when he came. This is one of the most helpful passages in Scripture to enable us to understand the workings of the Holy Spirit in our day, in our generation. He says to them:

> *And when he comes, he will convince the world of sin and of righteousness and of judgment* [The ministry of the Spirit to the world is to convince them of these three things.]: *of sin, because they do not believe in me; of righteousness, because I go to the Father, and you will see me no more; of judgment, because the ruler of this world is judged.*   John 16:8-11

I wonder if there is any passage of Scripture more frequently misread than that one. It is very commonly quoted, and is usually understood to say that the Holy Spirit will come into the world and work directly upon the hearts of unbelievers, those who are not Christians, and convict them, or convince them, of these three things: sin, righteousness, and judgment. But that is not what it is saying. Let's read it again, together with the preceding verse, emphasizing a key word. And I want to take that same word and insert it in verse eight where it does not occur, but where the context

makes clear that it belongs. I think you will see what
I mean. Jesus says (note emphases added):

> *Nevertheless I tell you the truth: it is to your
> advantage that I go away, for if I do not go
> away, the Counselor will not come to you; but
> if I go, I will send him to you. And when he
> comes* [to you], *he will convince the world of
> sin and of righteousness and of judgment.*
>   John 16:7, 8

You see, the Holy Spirit is not coming to the world; he
is coming to you, to the church, to the Christian. And
when he comes to the Christian, this will convince the
world of sin and of righteousness and of judgment.
That is what he is saying. In fact, Jesus had already
said specifically to his disciples that when the Spirit
of truth would come, the world would not be able to
receive him. It does not receive him—it cannot receive
him—because it neither sees him or knows him (*see*
John 14:17). Therefore he does not come to the world;
he comes to us. But when he comes to us and operates
in us as he intends, he will have this threefold effect
upon the world.

There are three things the world ought to see when
it looks at the church. If it does not see these three
things, then the church is not a Spirit-filled church. It
is not operating in the way it is intended. You can
bring that down to the individual as well. There are
three things the world ought to see when it looks at
you as a Christian. If it does not see these three things,
then you are not filled with the Spirit. You are not
being led by, and operating by means of the Spirit of
God, as the Lord intended for you to do.

The Church Doesn't Save Anybody

The first thing the world ought to see when it looks
at us is that the issue of life is Jesus. It ought to be
convicted of sin—*because they do not believe in me.* I
am convinced that if the church had not reflected
Jesus and spoken of him the world would soon have
forgotten him. In fact, by now he would have become
some dim name in history, for the world desperately

wants to forget that Jesus ever came and lived among us. It desperately wants to relegate his name and all his teachings to the farthest reaches of ancient history and to forget about him. If you do not believe that, just listen to some of the teachers of today. They tell you that undoubtedly Jesus was a great man, but he lived in the far distant past. What he said has no relevancy to our day and so we need not be concerned about him. What is the church for? It is to bring Jesus consistently before the world. It is no accident that the great spiritual awakening of our day, in which the Spirit has been moving in great power, has been labeled the Jesus Movement. That is what the church ought to be doing—constantly talking about Jesus.

When I travel around the country I visit many different churches. And so many times I find that the thing most emphasized by the church, in its attempts to reach out to the world, is the church! The church presents the program of the church, and what the church will do, and offers the church to society. The early Christians never wasted their time in such things. They never talked about the church; they talked about the Lord. The church doesn't save anybody. The church doesn't help anybody. It is the Lord who does it. He redeems, he changes, he revolutionizes, he forgives, he restores, he heals—not the church! When the church is Spirit-filled it talks about Jesus. And when the world hears that, then it is finally convinced that its most basic and fundamental sin is not the evil things it does, but the fact that it does not believe in Jesus.

The second thing of which they are to be convinced is righteousness, Jesus says—*because I go to the Father, and you will see me no more.* That is, when the world looks at the church it ought to see a different way of life, a different standard of behavior. What it once saw in Jesus it is now to see in the church. And this is what convinces the world that there are absolutes in life. Secular writers and philosophers will tell you that there are no absolutes, no standards. Whatever anyone wants to do is right for him to do. There is nothing inherently right or wrong; it is only good or bad in terms of how it affects an individual. We are deluged

today by *situational ethics*, the idea that the situation
alone determines whether a thing is right or wrong.
And the world will believe that until it sees in the
church a standard of behavior which makes it realize
that some things are always helpful, but that others
always blast and ruin, that there is clear-cut righteousness and there is absolute evil.

A Different Kind of Beauty

Not long ago, during the Body Life service at our
church, there was some wonderful sharing, a wonderful openness, and a sense of the Lord's presence at
work, which could be seen in our love and concern for
one another. I met a man afterward who was standing
on the platform looking out over the congregation as
people were talking and sharing and visiting and
praying. He shook his head and said, "I don't understand this. I can't get over it. All these young people
—what do they want to come here for? I don't understand." I said, "It's because here they can hear the
truth. And there is one thing young people want more
than anything else—truth, honesty, reality, the way
things are. Here they can hear it, and it is truth about
Jesus." He said, "Well, maybe so. I'll say one thing:
these are the most beautiful young people I've ever
seen."

That is what the world ought to see when it looks at
the church: beauty. It is what the Old Testament calls
the beauty of holiness. When the Word of God is fulfilled, and the Lord Jesus is reigning in an individual's
life, and that person is obedient to the Lord and to his
Word, there is a beauty about that life which captures
attention. It is righteousness, the beauty of holiness,
and it captivates others. They understand there *is*
a difference, and they want to be like that.

The third thing the world is to see as it looks at the
church is judgment—*because the ruler of this world is
judged*. As they look at the church they ought to see
that a head-on clash is coming, between the philosophy
of the world and the philosophy of Jesus Christ, and
that the One who is going to win is Jesus. All that the
world lives by will ultimately be demolished, destroyed.
A judgment is coming. And the sign of it to the

world is that the power of Satan is already broken
in the lives they are observing. Here are people who
live by different standards. They follow a different
system of morals. They know how to love, how to
reach out. They no longer are tied up in themselves,
bound up within, tortured by tensions and fears. This
is not seen perfectly in any one of us, but the world
sees it beginning and growing and happening, and it
shows them that the power of evil is broken, that the
prince of this world is judged, that this is the goal
toward which history is moving. This is what the world
is to see when it looks at the church. But it is only
when the church is living this way that the world can
see it. If they don't see it, it is because we are denying
the reality of that judgment.

Our Lord moves on to speak of how the Spirit himself will work in the believer, with each of us. This is
an extremely helpful passage.

> *I have yet many things to say to you, but you
> cannot bear them now. When the Spirit of truth
> comes, he will guide you into all the truth; for
> he will not speak on his own authority, but
> whatever he hears he will speak, and he will
> declare to you the things that are to come. He
> will glorify me, for he will take what is mine and
> declare it to you. All that the Father has is mine;
> therefore I said that he will take what is mine
> and declare it to you.*   John 16:12–15

There is the teaching of the Spirit to each believer.
The primary fulfillment of this, of course, was to the
disciples themselves. It was the process by which the
rest of the Scriptures were given. As this was fulfilled
in the apostles' lives, they were led by the Spirit to
speak the truth which is recorded here in the pages of
the New Testament—the Gospels, the Epistles, and the
Book of Revelation. Some even see these divisions in the
words of verse 13. *When the Spirit of truth comes, he
will guide you into all the truth*—that would be the
Gospels. *He will not speak on his own authority, but
whatever he hears he will speak*—there are the
Epistles. *He will declare to you the things that are to
come*—that would be the Book of Revelation.

How Comes Before *What*

But I think the Lord means for us to understand
the process by which the Spirit himself is going to
teach us. First Jesus emphasizes the prerequisite to
learning. He says to these disciples: *I have yet many
things to say to you.* Why hasn't he said them? What
was hindering him? The answer, he says, is that they
couldn't bear them then. It would be laying too heavy
a load on them. It would be a demand greater than
they could fulfill, and so he refuses to lay it on them.
What was it they were lacking? They lacked the understanding of the resource upon which to draw. They
did not know how to handle these demands, how to
satisfy these requirements, and so Jesus would not
tell them these things until they had the power by
which to respond.

That is a very important consideration. Today there
are many conferences and seminars and meetings being held in which great biblical truth is being set
before people. But they are not always being told
how to respond to it. The only response they know is to
summon up their natural commitment and their natural strength and to try to do the best they can to fulfill
it. When that happens it always destroys people without their knowing why, because although what they are
told to do is right, they don't know how to respond to
it in the Spirit. It is important for us to understand
that you have to know how to respond by faith and trust
in the One who dwells within you, before you ever
learn of the demand which the truth of God makes
upon you. That is the prerequisite to learning.

Then Jesus goes on into the process, and the three
divisions he gives are most helpful. *When the Spirit
of truth comes, he will guide you into all the truth.*
The word he uses for *guide* means "conduct," like a
tour guide. I was recently in Hawaii and visited the
City of Refuge, the ancient site where the Hawaiian
kings had erected a city which, like the biblical cities
of refuge, was a place where those who accidentally
killed someone, or violated a taboo, could run from
revengeful relatives or avenging justice. Once they
had attained the shelter of the City of Refuge they
were safe from harm. Our guide took us around this

site and explained each feature, point by point. That is what is referred to here. The Holy Spirit will be like a tour guide. He will take you through the truth of the Word and the truth about life, and he will patiently and gradually explain to you what it is all about. Your level of understanding will rise as you go. In other words, the work of the Spirit will be to gradually unfold the truth in every individual's life. It is not going to be one big display in which you get it all in a six-week course. Rather, it is a gradual unfolding as you move through life, and a deepening level of understanding as you penetrate into truth until it begins to make sense.

The second aspect is that *he will not speak on his own authority, but whatever he hears he will speak.* What does Jesus mean? He means that the Spirit of God is never going to give you isolated truth. He will not come out with some startling, brand-new, absolutely different revelation which nobody has ever heard of before! Every now and then we hear of some preacher who says, "God has revealed to me this brilliant new idea. Nobody has ever taught it before. If you want to know the secret you've got to come to me!" That is exactly what Jesus says will *not* happen. The Spirit of God will never speak that way. He will speak only what he hears. The Spirit, as God, is always hearing what God is forever saying to men. Therefore, what he says is always integrated truth, always in line with what God has already said. It will never differ fom what he has said in the past, but will fit into the context of life as God has revealed it.

Truth and Consequences

The third division is: *He will declare to you the things that are to come.* Unquestionably this refers to the passages in our New Testament which predict our Lord's return and what will happen at the end of history to lead up to it—when the kingdoms of the earth will rise up and band together in enmity against the Lord, when persecution and violence and tribulation will break out upon the earth, when the man of sin will arise and rule with worldwide authority to put down all men and institutions which represent God, and to exalt man as god in God's place.

But it also means that the Spirit of God is going to be presenting truth in such a way—by means of the revelation of the Word and a gradual elevating of our understanding of it—that it will point to the consequences which lie ahead. It is consequential truth: it will open your eyes to where you are going. It will help your understanding of life to see what the results are going to be. Therefore the work of the Spirit is constantly to be making us aware of what lies ahead because of what we are doing now.

All of this is what the Spirit of God will be doing when he comes into the life of a believer. Our Lord ends with the point, the aim, of the teaching of the Spirit: *He will glorify me, for he will take what is mine and declare it to you.* Sometimes when you listen to Bible teachers today you get the idea that there is to be a kind of Jesus-oriented Bible teaching with which we begin the Christian life, but that as we grow a bit and mature we are to move on to Spirit-oriented truth, to recognize that the sign of maturity is to be concerned no longer with Jesus but with Spirit. Nothing could be further from the truth! The work of the Spirit is to glorify Jesus. The Spirit-filled life is the life in which Jesus is central. And the one who matures is the one who grows deeper in his understanding of Jesus. "For the Spirit will not speak of himself," Jesus says, "but he will take what is mine and reveal it unto you."

Treasures of Wisdom

How vast is this range of teaching? Well, Jesus tells us in verse 15: *All that the Father has is mine*—the Spirit is going to take the things of mine and reveal them unto you, and all that the Father has is mine. *Therefore I said that he will take what is mine and declare it to you.* A young man asked me the other day, "Is it right for a Christian to study secular subjects which have nothing to do with the Bible?" My answer was: "Paul tells us: *All things are yours, ... and you are Christ's; and Christ is God's* (1 Corinthians 3:22, 23). And in Colossians, Paul says of Jesus Christ: *In* [him] *are hid all the treasures of wisdom*

and knowledge (Colossians 2:3). As you investigate
any realm of science or knowledge or truth, if you do
in reliance upon the indwelling life of Jesus and the
teaching of the Spirit of God, he will open that branch
of truth to you. More and more you will begin to understand and see the things God has hidden there."

Remember the story of George Washington Carver,
that brilliant scientist who taught at the Tuskegee Institute in Alabama. He was born a slave, but he managed
to get an education as a scientist. He said on one occasion that the hunger of his heart was to discover the
secrets of the universe. "But," he said, "God said to
me, 'George, that's too big for you. I've got something
more your size. You take a peanut and work on that.' "
And so he began to investigate what God has hidden in
a peanut. He found over 330 different products which
could be made from the peanut, revolutionized the tech-
nology of his day, and became a tremendous leader
among the American people. But he always remained
a simple, Bible-believing, humble servant of God who
relied upon God to open his mind to truth, in whatever
field it lay. "All things are yours. All the power of God
is yours." That is what Jesus means. "All that the
Father has is mine, and it will be made available to
you through the Spirit."

For millennia the Colorado River has been grinding
its way down through the Grand Canyon, on through
Arizona, and on its way to the Gulf of California. For
centuries men lived and died alongside that river—
starved to death, froze to death, shivered, sat in darkness—all for lack of power. Yet one of the most pow-
erful rivers in America was flowing by. But its power
was unavailable—until one day some men built Hoover
Dam. They erected this tremendous dam at great sacrifice of money and even of life, but for the first time
the power of the river was made available to man.

No Spectacular Flash

That is something like what happened at Calvary.
All the power of God was there, flowing around man,
but unavailable—until the cross of Jesus Christ. At
the cross, at enormous sacrifice, the power of God was
released to man. Yet it was still too much. As you drive

across the Mojave Desert between Arizona and Los Angeles you see the great transmission towers which bring the power of Hoover Dam into the Los Angeles basin. Every one of them bears a warning sign: DANGER—HIGH VOLTAGE. Energy is streaming through that wire at hundreds of thousands of volts. But how can you use a hundred thousand volts? It is too much. So a system of transformers has been installed which breaks it down until it comes out at levels we can use —110 volts, 220 volts—whatever it takes. By this means all the power generated at Hoover Dam is now available for people to use in Southern California. Something like that is what is in view here. I like to read Jesus' statement this way:

It is better for you that I go away, for if I do not go away, the Transformer will not come to you; but if I go, I will send him to you. And when he, the Transformer, comes, he will make available to you all the limitless forces which lie in me. He will take what is mine, and give it to you in quantities that you can handle, just right for your situation. For back of him lies all the limitless power of God.

That is what he is teaching us. That is what the world is waiting to see in our lives—power, coming not in some spectacular flash which startles and scares everybody, but released in useful quantity. That's what I need. I'm like these disciples—a brother to them. I cannot bear the full revelation of the love and grace of Jesus Christ. I need to have it broken down to my size. But it is there, ready for me to take, ready for me to use in my situation. That is available to each of us.

He will glorify me, for he will take what is mine and declare it to you. So that the world, looking at us, can see the sin of not believing in Jesus. He is the issue. So that they can see the righteous conduct which God alone can produce in a life. So they can know that God is still in control of history, that all of history is trending toward one great event which lies yet in the future. So they can see in us that quality of life which makes life worth the living. That is what the Spirit of God has come to do.

Lord Jesus, we thank you for the truth of these words, that this is what you are doing today—to the end that the world in its blindness and darkness may see you, Lord of Life, Lord of Glory, the One in whom are hidden all the treasures of wisdom and knowledge, the key and secret to life itself, and that they may come to you and receive life at your hand. We thank you for that life, and for the power given to us by the Holy Spirit. Help us to walk in these ways. In his name. Amen.

tern rolling on into joy. When a woman is in
travail she has sorrow because her hour has
come, but when she is delivered of the child, she

9

The Abiding Principles
John 16:16-33

While Jesus talks to his disciples about the work of
the Spirit—the Strengthener who is to come and live
within them—they are passing through the vineyards
on the slopes of Mount Zion, coming around the city
walls into the very shadow of the Temple. As this talk
is coming to a close, they are about to cross over the
Kidron Valley and make their way up the Mount of
Olives into the darkness of Gethsemane's Garden. At
this point our Lord resumes a conversational style in
his address to them. It interests me to watch Jesus
with his disciples and to observe his methods of teaching. Sometimes he speaks rather formally and at some
length, as in the Sermon on the Mount. But here he
intersperses these periods of formal teaching with
opportunities for questions and discussion. He is so
anxious to clear up their fears that he now gives them
an opportunity to break in with questions.

*"A little while, and you will see me no more;
again a little while, and you will see me." Some
of his disciples said to one another, "What is
this that he says to us, 'A little while, and you
will not see me, and again a little while, and you
will see me'; and, 'because I go to the Father'?"
They said, "What does he mean by 'a little
while'? We do not know what he means." Jesus
knew that they wanted to ask him; so he said to
them, "Is this what you are asking yourselves,
what I meant by saying, 'A little while, and you
will not see me, and again a little while, and you
will see me'? Truly, truly, I say to you* [that is
the mark of great significance in the words of
Jesus], *you will weep and lament, but the world
will rejoice; you will be sorrowful, but your*

114

sorrow will turn into joy. When a woman is in travail she has sorrow, because her hour has come; but when she is delivered of the child, she no longer remembers the anguish, for joy that a child is born into the world. So you have sorrow now, but I will see you again and your hearts will rejoice, and no one will take your joy from you."
                                            John 16:16-22

Notice that the concern of the disciples here is over how long this absence is going to last. Jesus has said: *A little while, and you will see me no more,* and his disciples have immediately picked up that phrase, "a little while." Their hearts clutch with fear, they say to themselves, "How long does he mean?" And their attention is also on his words, "because I go to the Father." They ask, "Why does this have to happen? What does he mean, 'because I go to the Father' ?" The focus of their concern is on *When?* and *Why?*

If you and I had been there, that is exactly what we would have asked! We are always concerned about how long a trial is going to last, and about why we have to go through it anyway. Are these not the questions we inevitably ask whenever we have trouble—"Why?" and "How long?" But you notice that when Jesus answers the troubled disciples he ignores the whole matter of time. He repeats the questions, so they know he has heard what they asked, but he never answers their questions directly. His answer stresses the process, and the result which is certain to follow. In other words, Jesus isn't concerned with the *Why?* and *How long?* but with the *How?* and the *What?* He makes clear to them that a period of sorrow is inevitable. He cannot spare them, cannot save them from it. There will be a time when they will weep and lament and be in sorrow, and when the world around will be rejoicing. "But," he says, "your sorrow will be turned into joy." How long it takes is not significant; the inevitable result is the important thing.

Not Replaced, but Transformed

That is a very important lesson to learn. When I say to the Lord, "How long, how long do I have to go

through this?" the Lord's emphasis is strictly upon
what is coming at the end, the joy which is certain. To
illustrate this, our Lord uses the beautiful figure of
childbirth. A mother goes through a time of sorrow
when her child is being born, but later she experiences
a time of joy when the baby is delivered.

In the morning service at our church, at the times
when babies are dedicated, the faces of the mothers are
always a picture of joy. They are "turned on" with the
gladness of that moment. What is causing the joy?
The baby. Yet, a few weeks before, those same mothers
were in anguish and pain, and their faces pictured
that anguish. And what was causing the pain? The
baby. In other words, the same thing which caused the
sorrow would later be the cause of the joy.

That is different from what we usually think. Most
of us assume that our sorrow is going to be *replaced*
by joy. But the promise of Jesus is that the very thing
which caused the sorrow is also going to be the cause
of the joy. That is a revelation of one of the great
principles which mark authentic Christianity, one of
the ways by which our Lord works in our life. He takes
the very thing which causes us heartache and sorrow,
and turns it into a cause of joy. That is most remarkable!

And God doesn't care how long it takes. We do, but
he doesn't. He is anxious only for the increase of joy.
And that joy will come from within. It will not be due
to the circumstances. As Jesus has made clear all along,
it will be due to the presence of the Holy Spirit within.

Recently I read an account of the life of Dr. R. A.
Torrey, one of the great Bible teachers of a past generation and founder of the Bible Institute of Los Angeles. Dr. and Mrs. Torrey went through a time of
great heartache when their twelve-year-old daughter
died. The funeral was held on a gloomy, miserable,
rainy day—dismal and melancholy. They stood around
this forlorn little grave and watched as the body of
their little girl was put away. As they turned away,
Mrs. Torrey said, "I'm so glad Elisabeth is with the
Lord, and not in that box." But even knowing this to
be true, their hearts were broken.

Dr. Torrey said that the next day, as he was walking

down the street, the whole thing broke over him anew —the loneliness of the years ahead without her presence, the heartbreak of an empty house, and all the other implications of her death. He was so burdened by this that he looked to the Lord for help. And I want to share his words with you:

And just then this fountain, the Holy Spirit, that I had in my heart, broke forth with such power as I think I had never experienced before, and it was the most joyful moment I had ever known in my life! Oh, how wonderful is the joy of the Holy Ghost! It is an unspeakably glorious thing to have your joy not in things about you, not even in your most dearly loved friends, but to have *within* you a fountain ever springing up, springing up, springing up, always springing up three hundred and sixty-five days in every year springing up under all circumstances unto everlasting life!

That is what Jesus is talking about here. The alchemy of the Spirit is to take the thing which causes pain and to transmute it until it causes joy. It may take some time. It is a process. There will be sorrow and tears and lamenting. But eventually it will turn into joy. *Your sorrow will turn into joy.*

In His Name

Now, what releases this joy? Well, Jesus tells us. For the third time in this discourse, he repeats the promise of answered prayer:

In that day you will ask me no questions. Truly, truly, I say to you, if you ask anything of the Father, he will give it to you in my name. Hitherto you have asked nothing in my name; ask, and you will receive, that your joy may be full.   John 16:23, 24

The process which leads to joy is a trustful prayer, a resting upon God to answer your need. This is why our Lord has underscored this for the third time. It will be the Triune God who works, therefore prayer is to be addressed to the Father, by the Spirit, in the name of the Son, and will no longer be addressed to Jesus alone.

"In that day you will ask nothing of me." The key, of course, is the phrase—*in my name: ask ... in my name.* I have mentioned this in an earlier chapter, but I want to expand somewhat on it now. *In my name* means at least three things.

In my name means, first, asking in line with our Lord's objectives. To ask in anyone's name means to ask as though you were that person. This means we are to ask for what Jesus would want, what he is after, and not for our own desires. Prayer is not a means by which you get God to do what you want, but rather, it is a means by which God does through you what he wants, and it is a very necessary part of the process that you pray. James tells us: ... *You do not have, because you do not ask* (James 4:2). Prayer is an integral part of that process. We *must* ask. But James also says: *You ask and do not receive, because you ask wrongly, to spend it on your passions* (James 4:3). Rather, it is to be for the objective which God has in your life.

Now, that permits a vast range of prayer! There are many things God wants you to have, and you have every right to ask. This covers material things as well as spiritual blessings. Jesus taught us to pray, "Give us this day our daily bread," and there is nothing wrong with that. There is nothing wrong with asking for other material needs. Some people get the idea that prayer is just for spiritual blessings, but that is not so. But what you ask must further the objectives God has in mind.

Second, to pray in Jesus' name means an acceptance of the process by which God works, and which Jesus relied upon. That process, as we know, is the cross and the resurrection—that is, a cross which represents the end, the hopelessness of everything else, and a resurrection beyond it, beyond what could possibly be anticipated by men. That is the way God works. He is a God of Resurrection!

That is why God often pushes us to the very limit before our prayers are answered. We cry out, "Lord, why don't you answer? If you would just step in *now* you could stop all this tragedy which is occurring!" But God sometimes doesn't stop tragedy. He is a master of brinkmanship. He pushes you right to the brink, sometimes over the brink, in order that out of what appears to be an absolutely hopeless condition, from man's point of view, he may restore the whole thing.

This is the kind of God you are dealing with. You can expect him to act this way because this is what he says he will do: *For my thoughts are not your thoughts, neither are your ways my ways, says the Lord* (Isaiah 55:8). And Peter reminds us: *Beloved, do not be surprised at the fiery ordeal which comes upon you to prove you, as though something strange were happening to you* (1 Peter 4:12). No, no; this is God's way of working. If he pushes you to the brink, don't be surprised, for resurrection lies beyond.

The third element of praying in Jesus' name is to pray in dependence upon his performance, upon his activity. It is Jesus who will do these things. He says so! *Whatever you ask in my name, I will do it, that the Father may be glorified in the Son* (John 14:13). It is not done by our scurrying around trying to arrange things and work them out for ourselves. It is done by our reliance upon him to carry it through in his own unique way. Therefore, to ask in Jesus' name is to consent to those three elements of prayer. That is the way joy is brought to the full, the way sorrow is turned to joy.

Direct to You

In the next section our Lord underscores another great principle by which the Christian life is to be lived:

I have said this to you in figures; the hour is coming when I shall no longer speak to you in figures but tell you plainly of the Father. In that day you will ask in my name; and I do not say to you that I shall pray the Father for you; for the Father himself loves you, because you have loved me and have believed that I came from the Father. I came from the Father and have come into the world; again, I am leaving the world and going to the Father.

John 16:25–28

Up to this point in the disciples' lives, they have been
very much aware of this marvelous, unique relationship which Jesus has with his Father. They have noted
that he has a dependence upon the Father, a trust of
the Father, and a fellowship and communion with the
Father which they know nothing about. They have
relied upon Jesus to obtain for them privilege and
favor with the Father. "But now," Jesus says, "that
must end. You are no longer to look upon yourselves
as separated from the Father, nor to think that I have
a special link with him which you cannot know. This is
now brought to an end, for the Father himself loves
you directly, just as he loves me."

And notice why—not because you behaved, but because you believed. That is so important! I find very
many Christians who really feel that God owes them
something because they have behaved well, have tried
to do what he says. They feel that if they live a good,
clean, moral life, God therefore owes them some special treatment. I am tempted this way myself, as I am
sure you are. When trouble strikes, I have heard people
say, "Why should this happen to *me?* How come God
sent this to *me?* What have *I* done to deserve this?"
Most of us are ready to cry out to God, "It's not fair,
Lord! Here I've been working for you and helping you
out, and this is the way you treat me! It's not fair!"
But, you see, it isn't on the basis of your behavior that
God loves you; he loves you because you believe. You
believe in Jesus. And on that basis his love is manifested as a Father's love—*directly* to you. We used to
sing in Sunday school,

Near, so very near to God, nearer I could not be;
For in the Person of His Son, I'm just as near as He.
Dear, so very dear to God, dearer I could not be;
The love with which He loved His Son, such is His love
    for me.

That is what Jesus wants us to know. We have a direct
relationship with the Father, and his love toward us is
as it was toward Jesus. He loves us!

Not long ago, I had the joy of having my young
daughter travel with me, and we spent a lot of time

together. We studied and prayed and read together, and played together, and just had a great time! I seized the occasion to teach her how to get up in the morning. Do you fathers ever teach your children how to get up in the morning? Not only to get up, but *how* to get up? There is a threefold technique in getting up: first, we stretch. That gets the body going. Then, smile. That puts the soul in the right attitude, so that we don't start the day grumbling. And then say, "God loves me." Because that sets the spirit right. You are reminding yourself of your identity in that way. Thus in body, soul, and spirit, you are starting the day right. Stretch, smile, and say, "God loves me." That is what Jesus is saying here. The second great source of security in the Christian life is this remarkable love which the Father has for us as individuals. The Father loves us!

Peace in Jesus

The last division stresses a third word:

His disciples said, "Ah, now you are speaking plainly, not in any figure! Now we know that you know all things, and need none to question you; by this we believe that you came from God." Jesus answered them, "Do you now believe? The hour is coming, indeed it has come, when you will be scattered, every man to his home, and will leave me alone; yet I am not alone, for the Father is with me. I have said this to you, that in me you may have peace. In the world you have tribulation; but be of good cheer, I have overcome the world."

John 16:29–33

Notice that the security of these disciples rested on the ability they thought they had to understand what he was saying to them. They wanted to *know,* and then they thought they would feel at peace. "Now we know," they said "now we understand." Jesus had been speaking to them in figures—the vine and the branches, the washing of the feet, the woman in childbirth—these illuminating figures. "But now you're speaking to us plainly. Now we know and understand that you are indeed from God." They felt a sense of security because they understood that.

That is so like us! We think that God has to explain what we're going through, and that then we'll feel secure. Our peace wants to rest upon a certain knowledge of what is happening. But our Lord is very careful here to point out that this kind of peace is very insecure indeed. "Within an hour you will be running like a bunch of frightened sheep. You say you know who I am. You say you understand that I came from God and that I know all things. Do you know that within an hour's time you will be so confused and so uncertain of what is happening you will run away and leave me alone? Rather than trusting me to work things out, you'll forsake me and not want to be identified with me.

"And yet I'll not be alone. My security won't be threatened in that hour, for the Father is with me. And I say this to you in order that you might know the kind of peace I have. It is not based on what happens, or even on my understanding of what happens, but upon a trust in the One who controls what happens. I say this to you, that in me you may have peace. In the world you're going to have nothing but trouble— trouble at work, trouble at school, trouble in your home, trouble in your family. You'll have nothing but trouble, because that is the way this world is. But be of good cheer. I am in control of the world. I have overcome the world."

Isn't that an encouraging word? These words have meant a great deal to me in these past few months and years. I've been going through a time of great personal stress, times of deep sorrow, times of great pressure, times of uncertainty and lack of understanding, not knowing what God is working out, perceiving him to be working in ways which I have thought were utterly wrong, thinking he had no business doing things like this to me. And I've had to rest upon these tremendous revelations of his Word, and upon these marvelous summary words—*love, joy, peace*. They are the fruit of the Spirit, aren't they?

His joy—despite circumstances—sorrow turned into

joy. His love—the Father's own love, the Father's tender care, lovingly apportions to each day that which he wants for you. I so enjoyed hearing again recently the words of that old song, "Day By Day." I had forgotten the words, and they hit with new and fresh power:

> Day by day and with each passing moment,
>   Strength I find to meet my trials here,
> Trusting in my Father's wise bestowment,
>   I've no cause for worry or for fear.
> He whose heart is kind beyond all measure
>   Gives unto each day what he deems best,
> Lovingly, its part of pain and pleasure,
>   Mingling toil with peace and rest.
>   LINA SANDELL

That is the work of the Father. And then this last word—peace. "You can have my peace," Jesus says, "my sense of security, which rests not in the circumstances, not in the understanding of the circumstances which we so crave, but in a confidence that the One who is guiding the circumstances knows what he is doing." That is where peace comes from.

Then he leaves his disciples, and us, with these words, and begins to pray. We will look at that prayer next, but he ends this discourse with these great, abiding words: joy, love, peace.

———————

Our Father, we thank you for your love for us. We thank you that you are our Father, and that you love us directly, as Jesus said; that we are precious to you, as he was precious to you; that your eye is ever upon us, as it was upon him; and that you are ever alert to our cry, always aware of our need. But we know that just as he passed through times of great pressure, times of disappointment, times of betrayal, times of heartbreak and sorrow, agony, and lack of understanding, so we, too, Lord, must pass through them. But we are upheld, knowing that your promise is, "Your sorrow shall be turned into joy." We thank you for that peace which passes understanding, which we do not know how to explain, but which is there as we trust a Father's hand, a Father's heart, to guide us through. As we go through times of pressure, we pray that you will sustain and strengthen us, and lead us out into that broad and wide place unto which you go. We ask in Jesus' name. Amen.

10

The Accomplishments of Jesus
John 17:1-8

We have reached the climax in our study of the Upper Room Discourse as we look at the prayer with which our Lord concludes. It is probably one of the most profound passages in all the New Testament, and volumes have been written about this one chapter alone. Our Lord and his disciples have come to the edge of the Kidron Valley, and are about to cross over into the shadows of Gethsemane's Garden. It is here that our Lord begins his prayer. It is evident that he prays aloud in order that the disciples may hear what he has to say to the Father. After they have entered the Garden he withdraws from the disciples and goes off by himself and prays in private to the Father. But *here* his prayer is public, so that we might hear his communion.

The prayer falls into three general divisions, which we will take in three separate chapters, as we attempt to get as much as we can from the depths of this prayer—although, as John R. Stott says so eloquently in *Christ the Liberator*, "The best we can do is but to paddle in its shallows." Our Lord prays for three things: first, he prays for himself, that he might be glorified (verses 1-8); then he prays for his disciples, that they might be sanctified (verses 9-19); and then he prays for the whole church down through the ages, that it might be unified (verses 20-26). The introduction to the prayer is given in the first two verses:

When Jesus had spoken these words, he lifted up his eyes to heaven and said, "Father, the hour has come; glorify thy Son that the Son may glorify thee, since thou hast given him power over all flesh, to give eternal life to all whom thou hast given him."   John 17:1, 2

125

The first request of Jesus is that he might be glorified.
"Well," you say, "isn't that a selfish request?" If we
prayed it, yes, it would be. If we prayed that we would
be exalted or magnified or glorified in order that the
world might see how important we were, it would indeed be a selfish request. But you notice that our Lord
immediately adds: ... *that the Son may glorify thee.*
So the ultimate end of his request for glory is that the
Father may be glorified.

This is always the ultimate purpose for all existence:
that it might glorify God. Your life has no value except
as it glorifies God. As we have seen earlier in this discourse, to glorify someone means to manifest or display their hidden virtue or wisdom or power or beauty,
to bring out that which is hidden away in them. And
here our Lord is asking that he be glorified, that is,
that things hidden in him—resources and wisdom and
beauty which are rightfully his—might now be made
manifest, in order that he in turn might manifest the
beauty and the glory and the order and the wisdom of
the Father. In reading this you can see that the major
work of all three Persons in the Godhead—Father,
Son, and Holy Spirit—is to display the mutual glory
of one another.

Our Lord now tells us why he needs this additional
glory. The Father has already glorified him, and will
glorify him again in his death. But the Lord, evidently,
is looking on beyond the cross. And he needs additional glory for the reason he gives in verse 2: *since
thou hast given him power over all flesh, to give eternal life to all whom thou hast given him.* That is why
he needs it—in order to fulfill the additional work
which was given him—that of giving eternal life to all
whom God has called.

The Great Task of God

There is something very significant here. Our Lord
is pointing out that in his Resurrection and Ascension
he will have, and does have, power over all flesh. That
means he is in charge of all things. As he himself says
just before he ascends to the Father: *All authority in
heaven and on earth has been given to me* (Matthew
28:18). The writer of Hebrews says that the Son up-

holds the universe by the Word of his power (*see* Hebrews 1:3). So here it is evident Jesus is aware that he is Lord over all the universe.

Jesus is Lord, whether men know it or not. That means he controls all the events of history—and all the ordinary events of our circumstances, our everyday lives. I have to believe that he allowed me to slip from a ladder yesterday and injure my foot because of some value he knew the experience would have for me. And I do believe that. I believe that all events are ordered by the Lord. He uses even the animosity and hatred of Satan against the human race in order to accomplish his purposes and his will.

During a meeting not long ago, we heard a very illuminating and helpful study from our missionary friends on China—what China is doing these days, where it is going, so far as anyone can tell, and what China is like today. Some of us were startled a bit when our friend read from Isaiah's prophecy the words of God concerning Cyrus, the pagan king of Persia, whom he would raise up (*see* Isaiah 44:24—45:6). God describes in detail how he would use him to put down nations and overthrow thrones and overpower kingdoms, *although Cyrus did not know God personally*. Our friend drew a very vivid parallel between Cyrus and Mao Tse-tung, illustrating the fact that God has used Mao in China and in the world to accomplish his purpose.

That is what our Lord means when he says here that he has power over all flesh, over all the nations—power to regulate their affairs, power to raise them up and put them down, power to shut doors so that a nation can be closed off from hearing the Gospel in order to sharpen its desire for it, while other nations are allowed to be open to hear the Gospel. All the events of history, all the events reported in our newspapers have been allowed by the Lord as he regulates and runs the affairs of earth, in order, as he says here, to give eternal life to all those whom God has given him.

The focal point of all human history is right here. Every event finds its significance only as it contributes in one way or another to the great task God has come into the world to do: to give eternal life to men and women. By virtue of the power he has to regulate the affairs of human history, he gives eternal life to those whom the Father calls and brings to the Son. Now, that is the Christian world view, and I think we need continually to bear it in mind these days—Jesus is Lord. This is not merely looking forward to a day when he will come again and reign as Lord; he already reigns as Lord over all the affairs of earth, and he is bringing them to the culmination which the Scriptures describe. Here he is aware of that fact, and in order to do this, he says, he needs additional glory.

An Infinite Undertaking

Have you ever tried to define eternal life? You say you were given eternal life. What do you mean? That you are going to be living in heaven forever? That is a phase of it, but that is not really what it is. What does it mean to have eternal life? Jesus defines it for us:

And this is eternal life, that they know thee the only true God, and Jesus Christ whom thou has sent.   **John 17:3**

Eternal life is the ability, the right, to know God in an ever-expanding, ever-increasing way, to understand and fellowship with, and be in close contact with this mighty Being who upholds all things by the Word of his power, and with Jesus Christ, who is the only way be which men can know God. That is eternal life —the knowledge of a Person.

This really shouldn't be surprising to us. After all, this is the way many things in life are. For example, what is marriage? Is it just two people living together in a house, sharing the same salary, raising children, washing dishes and making beds, and expressing a little sex? Is that all marriage is? No, marriage is the knowledge of a person. That is what makes marriage rich and full. It isn't just living together; it is knowing each other, and coming more and more to know one another.

Many marriages grow stale because this process

ceases, and people do not continue learning more and more of what is in the other person. So many couples come to me thinking they have arrived, that they have found out all there is to know about each other, and so their marriage appears to them dull and boring. But they haven't arrived. The knowledge of a person is an infinite undertaking. What makes human life rich is the discovery of what is in one another, who we are, and the sharing of it. And what makes eternal life worth the living is the discovery of God, the knowledge of him.

And this is the great gift which only Jesus Christ can give. Notice how exclusive is his claim. It is Jesus who says: *No one comes to the Father, but by me* (John 14:6). Those of us who are Christians must never give up that doctrine. We must never be willing to put any other approach to God on the level of Jesus Christ. We must never say that any person other than Jesus can lead men to God. For Jesus himself says that this is the case. It is he who points out that, of all men who have ever appeared on earth, only he has the power to give the knowledge of God, and of himself, to human beings. This is the gift of eternal life.

Notice how God works within the Godhead. There is amazing reciprocity of action here. The Father gives the Son power over all flesh. Then he calls out of humanity those whom he wants. Then he brings them to the Son, and the Son gives them the power to know God and the power to know himself. There is an interplay of activity back and forth. Did you ever think of yourself as called by the Father? I think many of us are so caught up with our human experience of Christ that we forget God must call us before we even can come to him. As Jesus himself puts it: *No one can come to me unless the Father who sent me draws him* ... (John 6:44). These desires which we have to find out what life is all about, this hunger for forgiveness which awakens within us, our longing for fulfillment, the desire to have questions about the future answered, all of these are part of the drawing of the Father, by the Spirit—bringing us to the place where Jesus alone can give us the gift of eternal life. Have you come t that place?

Prayer Is Part of the Process

Now Jesus specifies the nature of the glory which he
requires to complete this work:

> *I glorified thee on earth, having accomplished
> the work which thou gavest me to do* [we will
> look at that in a moment]; *and now, Father,
> glorify thou me in thy own presence with the
> glory which I had with thee before the world
> was made.*   John 17:4, 5

Jesus is praying that he might resume now the full
manifestations of Deity. He had laid them aside when
he came into the world, taking upon himself the limitations of humanity. I think it is so helpful for us to
realize that when our Lord was here he did not go
around showing people how God behaved; he showed
them how man behaved—man indwelt by God, as God
intended man to be. And all that you see in Jesus, during the days of his flesh, is a perfect humanity. His
Deity was hidden. He didn't give it up—you can't give
up what you are—but he laid aside the exercise of it.
Now he is asking that the Father will restore to him
that expression of Deity which was properly his before
the world was made. By this he is praying for the
Resurrection, and the Ascension to follow—that the
Father would raise him from the dead in glory, and
then later cause him to ascend to heaven to be with
him as he was before the world was made. He needs
this in order to perform the work of giving eternal
life to all those whom the Father would bring to him
out of every succeeding generation. It is as God that
he gives us eternal life.

There is a tremendous lesson here about prayer. Was
it not already God's program that if the Son were
crucified he would be raised from the dead and ascend
into the heavens? Yet when the hour comes, Jesus
asks the Father to do this. He prays for this glory
which was already promised to him. This helps us a
great deal in understanding prayer. Many people say
to me, "Why should I pray? God has already program-
med my life. He knows what I'm going to do and what's
going to happen to me, so why should I ask him to do

anything? It's all going to happen anyway." That position totally ignores the revelation of the Scriptures that prayer is a part of the process by which God brings to pass what he has already proposed to do. If you do not ask, it will not happen because it breaks the link by which God proposes to bring it about. Therefore prayer is vital, and our Lord gives us this example. He prays for that which was already promised him. Prayer is always based upon the promises of God.

Eleven Men

Let us look now at these words: *I glorified thee on earth,* for here we see the basis of his request for additional glory. Our Lord says: *I glorified thee on earth, having accomplished the work which thou gavest me to do.* Having arrived at the cross, he has finished one work; now another is about to begin. And for that additional work he needs this additional glory, this return to his original status as the Son of God. But the reason he can ask for it now is that he has finished the work which God has given him to do. In the next few verses we have a wonderful look at Jesus' own evaluation of what he has accomplished. What was this work which God gave him to do, which he has now finished, and finished with satisfaction, so that he can ask for more glory to accomplish the further work which lays before him? He tells us what it is:

I have manifested thy name to the men whom thou gavest me out of the world; thine they were, and thou gavest them to me, and they have kept thy word.   John 17:6

That is one part of it. Now he gives another:

Now they know that everything that thou hast given me is from thee; for I have given them the words which thou gavest me, and they have received them and know in truth that I came from thee; and they have believed that thou didst send me.   John 17:7, 8

The work he came to do was twofold: "I manifested your name to the men whom you gave me" and "I have given them your words." And in saying that, he says, "I have accomplished the work which you gave me to do." There have been many books written about the life of Christ, and they are filled with commentary on the amazing things Jesus did—the multitudes which followed him, the miracles he performed, the crowds to which he witnessed, the healings, the compassionate words he uttered. But Jesus is saying here that all of that was designed to reach eleven men. And having reached them, he says, "I have finished the work thou gavest me to do." Isn't that amazing?

He says, first, "I manifested thy name to them." What does that mean? A name always stands for resources. Your name stands for everything you are and have. When Elaine Smith, of Great Falls, Montana, became my wife, she took my name, and she literally took me for all I had! It wasn't much. I had saved up one hundred dollars for our honeymoon. We spent it within the first three days—and we had to cash her bonds to get home! Even today when I sign a check, the entire Stedman fortune—all of two hundred dollars of it—is laid on the line! When Jesus said he had manifested the name of the Father, he was saying that he had revealed to these men the resources in God by which he lived. His attitude and his actions told the story. The way he reacted, the serenity of spirit he displayed, the calmness with which he faced crises, the compassion with which he dealt with the weak, the tenderness, the love in everything he did and said—they saw at last that the secret was that he was drawing on the Father. "As I live by means of the Father, so you shall live by means of me." They learned that great secret.

And the result was, as Jesus says: *They have kept thy word.* Doesn't that reveal something about us? Why is it that though we have the Word of God so abundantly, yet we often find ourselves not keeping it? The only answer is that we become victims of a paralysis of the will. We lose our motivation. We become listless and lethargic and dull. Why? Because we have failed to grasp the resources available to us. The way to keep the Word of God is to draw upon the life of

God, now made available to us in the Son, as the Father's life was available to him, and by which he lived. The first great task he came to accomplish was to show these men how he lived, by what means he acted.

The second was: *I have given them the words which thou gavest me, and they have received them and know in truth that I came from thee; and they have believed that thou didst send me.*

These convincing words are what he came to give his disciples. He came to teach eleven men a wholly different way of life, a totally, radically different approach to living. Read the words of Jesus and you can see this. Take the words of the Sermon on the Mount. Those opening words reveal an entirely different approach to life than anything the world knows: "Blessed are the poor in spirit, for theirs is the kingdom of heaven. Blessed are those who mourn, for they shall be comforted. Blessed, *blessed* are the persecuted. *Blessed* are the pure in heart, blessed are the merciful, and the peacemakers—for theirs is a resource which the world knows nothing about. The kingdom of God, and all its resources, are available to them" (*see* Matthew 5:1-11).

The Work of Incarnation

So he has described all this, and these disciples have caught on—finally! The amazing thing is that they have just barely caught on—just before these words are uttered. If you look back at chapter 16 you can see this: *His disciples said, "Ah, now you are speaking plainly, not in any figure! Now we know that you know all things, and need none to question you; by this we believe that you came from God"* (John 16:29, 30). And Jesus heaves a big sigh of relief and says, "Now I've finished the work which you gave me to do. Now they know. My words at last have convinced them!" This was the work he came to do—to convince eleven men. He isn't worried about the multitudes who left him and went back. He doesn't care how many he has healed who would no longer acknowledge his name. He is interested only in these eleven Galilean peasants. This is all he had to show for his work. But he says, "That's enough. They know two great things: they

know how I live, and they've heard my words. They
have described what that life is like, and that is all
they need to know. When the Spirit comes and makes
all this real to them, that will change the world!" And
he is satisfied now to go back, in order that he might
work through these men as the Father has worked
through him.

So here is the great program of God. Jesus now says,
"Father, I've finished that work. Now give me the
glory I had with you before the world was—so that as
God the Son, upholding all things by the Word of my
power, running every event of human life and working
out the entire program from beginning to end, I might
work through these to whom I have given eternal life,
and through all who shall later believe on me through
their word, in order that the great work which you
have designed for men—that a great company of
people from all ages and tribes and generations and
tongues, shall receive the knowledge of you: the gift
of eternal life." And God granted that request. Jesus
was raised from the dead, and he ascended into the
heavens in order that he might fulfill this work. I believe that is what is meant in Hebrews, when the
writer says:

> *In the days of his flesh, Jesus offered up prayers
> and supplications, with loud cries and tears, to
> him who was able to save him from death, and
> he was heard for his godly fear.*   **Hebrews 5:7**

Thus we have the great work of redemption going on
throughout the world since that day. Isn't this an
amazing program that God has? He works through incarnation—life implanted into people. And that life,
lived by them, in their circumstances, is what will
change the world. Let us never forget this, as we see
it manifested in Jesus Christ our Lord.

Lord Jesus, we count it a great privilege to bow the knee to you and proclaim you as Lord, to the glory of God the Father, even in this day of rejection, when much of the earth scorns your claims and men turn their backs upon your righteous law and refuse to heed your gracious word of invitation. Yet we thank you, Lord Jesus, that we've been drawn by the Father, drawn by the Spirit to you. You have given to us the gift of eternal life—"that we may know the only true God, and Jesus Christ whom thou hast sent." Father, we thank you for this, and ask your blessing upon us. May we be faithful to that Word and to that life which is within us. In Jesus' name. Amen.

11

Kept
John 17:9-19

As our Lord begins his great prayer which brings this passage of Scripture to a close, he prays first for the restoration of his powers of Deity—and thus, for his resurrection, ascension, and glorification. He prays next for his disciples, the eleven men gathered there with him who are the fruit of his ministry. This section is not only for them, however, but since they are representatives of us, it is for us as well. It begins:

> *I am praying for them; I am not praying for the world but for those whom thou hast given me, for they are thine; all mine are thine, and thine are mine, and I am glorified in them.*
>
> **John 17:9, 10**

Here you see the reason for our Lord's prayer for these eleven men, growing out of his great, heartfelt love and concern for them. He prays for them for the same reason that we pray for each other—because there is a love and a concern for one another. Our Lord loves these men, and not only them but all who, like them, would believe in his name.

He tells us three reasons why he loves them and is concerned for them. First, because they are *those whom thou has given me.* That is, they are the gift of the Father to the Son. All of us have something we have been given by someone we love. We treasure that gift—not only because of its intrinsic value but because it comes from someone who means much to us. Jesus, looking at these men, has guarded them and loved them and been concerned for them because they represent the Father's choice for him.

Choice Men

Here is a revelation of how God works in human lives. We have already seen something of it previously in this prayer. In all the universe, Jesus is the only One who has authority to give eternal life—the right to know God, this mighty, amazing, marvelous, attractive, magnificent Being who flung the worlds into existence and who designed us in all our human complexity. He is the One whom to know is to gain the greatest blessing in life. And the only One who has the right to give us that knowledge is Jesus. But Jesus says that the Father has a part in this, too. He draws certain ones to him. God is at work throughout our lives drawing us to him by various means. If you have a hunger for goodness, that is the drawing of the Father. If you have a passion for truth and honesty, that is the drawing of the Father. If you love the words of Jesus and are attracted by who he is and what he says, that is the drawing of the Father, moving in you to bring you to Christ that you might commit yourself to him. And these eleven men have been drawn in that way. It is to these that he now commits the ministry which he himself has had. So they are dear to him because they are given to him by the Father.

And then he says that they are dear because *all mine are thine, and thine are mine.* That is, not only has the Father given them to him, but now they are his, they belong to him. His concern reaches out to them because they are his property, his ownership. I frequently read these words in First Corinthians because I think they capture one of the greatest truths in Christian faith: . . . . *You are not your own; you were bought with a price* . . . (1 Corinthians 6:19, 20). You do not belong to yourself if you are a Christian; you belong to God. You haven't the right to run your life; he has. You haven't the right to make your own program and plans; he has. You are bought with a price. These men were bought with that price and belonged to him, and so they are dear to him.

The third reason is: *I am glorified in them.* They are choice men because in them Jesus sees the means by which all the glory which is his due will be manifested. Just as a coach is glorified by the ability of the

athletes he has trained, or a teacher by the achieve-
ments of the scholars who learn from him, so Jesus is
to be glorified by these men. They would be the way
by which the world would know who he is. That is what
history has proven, hasn't it? We have the Bible because of these eleven men. We read of Jesus because
of them. He has been glorified before the whole world
by these eleven men. So they are infinitely precious
and dear to him, and thus he prays for them.

Now, what does he pray? Notice that he prays three
things for them. He doesn't pray for the world, because none of these things could be true of the world.
He prays for the world later, on his cross: *Father,
forgive them; for they know not what they do* (Luke
23:34). But here he is praying for these men:

*. . . . Holy Father, keep them in thy name which
thou hast given me, that they may be one, even
as we are one.*   John 17:11

His first request is that they will be kept in unity. The
second is found in verse 15:

*I do not pray that thou shouldst take them out
of the world, but that thou shouldst keep them
from the evil one.*   John 17:15

His second request is that they be kept from destruction. And the third request is:

Sanctify them in the truth. . . .   John 17:17

These are the three things he prays for these men who
are dear to him: "Keep them in unity; keep them from
destruction by the evil one; and sanctify them by your
truth." Now let's look at them in more detail and in
context:

*And now I am no more in the world, but they
are in the world, and I am coming to thee. Holy
Father [notice that—Holy Father], keep them in
thy name, which thou hast given me, that they
may be one, even as we are one. While I was*

with them, I kept them in thy name, which thou
hast given me; I have guarded them, and none
of them is lost but the son of perdition, that the
scripture might be fulfilled. But now I am
coming to thee. . . .   John 17:11-13

It is because of this change of guardianship that
Jesus prays for these men. "I am no longer in the
world, Father, I am coming to you; so you must keep
them. For I have kept them while I was with them."
He makes that clear. He has kept them by the same
resource by which he now asks the Father to keep
them: *I kept them in thy name.* That stands for all
resources and power and wisdom and glory of God,
available to man. "I kept them by that resource. And
now you keep them, Father, by the same resource."

Quarrelsome Apostles

This was not easy to do. Read the record of the Gospels and you will see that these men did not get along
very well. They were easily divided, threatened with
schism many times. He prays that they may be kept
one, kept in unity. "For," he says, "I kept them that
way." The record shows that this was a very difficult
task to accomplish. They were fighting and quarreling
with one another, in competition with each other, always striving to get ahead of one another and to put
each other down. Remember how James and John laid
hold of their mother to ask a special favor of Jesus
before the others could get their word in. And remember how Peter and John were at odds with one another throughout the whole course of the apostolic
training period. You find them in rivalry until the day
of Pentecost. When the Spirit of God came, Peter and
John became friends, and they worked together from
then on. Their enmity was ended by the coming of the
Spirit.

So our Lord prays for them here that they may be
kept in this way. His was a difficult task: he has had
to rebuke them and reprove them and correct them,
spend nights in prayer for them. But he has kept them
by the name and authority of the Father from all at-
tacks upon their unity, so that even now, in the shadow

of the cross, they are eleven men still together. *"None of them is lost,"* he says, *but the son of perdition."*

Judas never was a member of that band, in one sense—he never was part of the apostolic unity. Some think that he was fated, compelled to be lost—that he never had a chance. But this is not the case. It was not his fate to be lost; it was his destiny. There is a difference between fate and destiny. Fate is what you are compelled to do, what you cannot help; destiny is what you find possible if you make the right choices. We speak of Men of Destiny. What do we mean? We mean that they make the right choices so that all the potential of their lives is fulfilled. But there are men and women and children who miss their destiny because of the choices they make. And Judas was one. Therefore Jesus calls him *the son of perdition,* who never made the right choices, and so was lost.

But these other men who began with the right choice were never lost; he kept them to the end. Now the positions of Jesus and the Father are about to be reversed. While he was in the flesh, Jesus kept them by the Father's name. Now he asks that the Father keep them in the Son's name, the name which the Father has given him. Thus Jesus commits them to the mercy of the Father through the days to come.

Two Kingdoms

Now Jesus prays his second request—that they may be kept from the evil one:

> *. . . and these things I speak in the world, that they may have my joy fulfilled in themselves. I have given them thy word; and the world has hated them because they are not of the world, even as I am not of the world. I do not pray that thou shouldst take them out of the world, but that thou shouldst keep them from the evil one. They are not of the world, even as I am not of the world.*   John 17:13–16

In this section our Lord indicates the great realm of controversy between himself and Satan, the realm in which Satan's activity is manifested—the world. Throughout this whole discourse you find two communities in view: the world—secular society, organized in its antipathy against God, seeking to avoid any contact with and dependence upon God; and the church —the body of Christ, God's family.

Every spirit of independence which says, "You've got what it takes in yourself," is a wordly spirit, and is therefore satanic. Every spirit which says, "You can shape your own life and make your own future," is a worldly spirit. Every spirit which says, "Things of comfort and enjoyment in this life are of far more importance than relationships with people and spiritual values," is a worldly spirit, a satanic element.

The Lord knows that there is this conflict. He calls a group out of the world—not to be separate from it (as we will see), but to be a different group. God always sees humanity divided into these two divisions. Sometimes they are called two kingdoms—the Kingdom of God and the kingdom of Satan. Sometimes they are regarded symbolically as two cities—Jerusalem and Babylon. But in any case, there are always two.

The world is Satan's realm. He is the god of this world, the ruler of it. He is the one whom people blindly and ignorantly worship when they worship money and fame and power and pleasure, and all such attractions of the world. Jesus, knowing the danger of the world, prays for these disciples. And he points out the reason why the world hates them. *These things I speak in the world, that they may have my joy fulfilled in themselves.* Here are men who have learned a source of joy which the world does not know how to produce. And this always bothers the world. It longs to control everything.

Frightened by Joy

Have you ever noticed how men are unhappy unless they can control every force at work in their lives? This is the philosophy of the world. This is why men desperately try to subdue nature and to conquer the universe. The world is frightened and threatened by any source of joy or happiness or peace which does not itself provide. That is why these men were hated, because they had a source of inner joy and strength which the world could not explain.

You find a good example of this in Paul's Letter to the Philippians:

> *Only let your manner of life be worthy of the gospel of Christ, so that whether I come and see you or am absent, I may hear of you that you stand firm in one spirit, with one mind striving side by side for the faith of the gospel, and not frightened in anything by your opponents.*   **Philippians 1:27, 28**

These are men and women who have learned to stand up against persecution and mockery and ostracism, and not to be frightened or put down, but to be filled with steadiness and joy. Paul goes on to say in verse 28: *This is a clear omen to them of their destruction* [the world is frightened by this kind of a resilient spirit], *but of your salvation, and that from God.*

And so the world hates Christians because they have a source of life the world cannot explain. Satan tries to destroy it, tries to ruin people's happiness, marriages, lives, homes, health—anything! The devil is a murderer and his aim is to blast, to damage, to destroy in any way he can, through the deceitfulness of the allurements and illusions of the world.

No Isolation

Jesus, knowing this, prays for these men. Notice what he prays—two very important things. He says first: *I do not pray that thou shouldst take them out of the world.* Isn't that amazing? I remember Dr. Lewis Sperry Chafer, president and founder of Dallas Theological Seminary, and my dear professor, saying that as a young preacher he had had great controversies with those who held the Arminian persuasion—that once you were saved you could be lost again. He would say to them, "If I believed as you do, I would erect a chopping block beside every altar. And as soon as anybody got saved, I'd pass them over and chop their heads off. It would be worth it, rather than seeing them lost again once they had become a part of Christ!"

In effect, that is what we do when we say to new believers, "Look, now that you are a Christian, get out of the world. Don't have anything to do with it. Avoid any contact with it, and don't ever get mixed up in it as long as you live." Now, it may be necessary at times for a young Christian to get away from the world for a while. But not to be removed from it! It is a violation of our Lord's prayer when we take ourselves out of the world and build ourselves a wholly Christian life "from the womb to the tomb," with Christian friends and Christian contacts—when we never go any place non-Christians go, but simply isolate ourselves. There are many places and many churches like that today. But the result is that the world is left without light—to fall into decay and darkness, with no help, no help at all.

But, on the other hand, our Lord is aware that these men need to be kept from the evil one. So he prays for this, and for protection against contamination by the world and all its deadly delusions. It is so easy to conform to the world, to identify with it, to seek its values and to measure your life by its standards. What a deadly thing that is! Our Lord is calling here for men and women who, like himself, can live in the midst of the world—right up to the hilt—friends of sinners and tax collectors and publicans and prostitutes—and yet not become contaminated by its life but instead be a source of release to those around.

How do you live that way, walking a tightrope between falling off on one side into isolation or on the other side into conformity to the world? Jesus' answer is in his last request:

Sanctify them in the truth; thy word is truth. As thou didst send me into the world, so I have sent them into the world. And for their sake I consecrate myself [sanctify myself—same word in Greek], *that they also may be consecrated* [sanctified] *in truth.*   **John 17:17-19**

I don't know what you think sanctification is. All too often it is thought of as kind of a religious fumigation process—you go through it once and you're *sanctified,* and nothing can ever touch you again. But that is false on the face of it. Scripture doesn't teach that, and neither does experience. Sanctification is a simple word which means to be set apart for a certain purpose, to be put to its intended use. When I selected my necktie this morning from a number of other ties, I sanctified it. When you selected the seat in which you are sitting, you sanctified that seat; you put it to its intended use. When you tear off a piece of paper to write a note, you sanctify that piece of paper to its intended use. That is all it means. And when God called these men, and you and me, to be Christians, he sets us apart for the use for which we were intended—not to be our own, but to be his instruments, and to walk in conformity with his ways.

Know the Truth

What is it which accomplishes this? Jesus tells us. It is the Word, the truth about life. The world lives in a continual shimmering illusion, a dream world. The world lives by what it thinks is truth, by values and standards which are worthless, but which the world esteems highly. Jesus said: ... *what is exalted among men is an abomination in the sight of God* (Luke 16:15). That is how the world lives. And how can we live in that kind of a world—touch it and hear it, have it pouring into our ears and exposed to our eyes day and night, and not be conformed to its image and squeezed into its mold?

The answer is, we must know the truth. We must know the world and life the way God sees it, the way it really is. We must know it so clearly and strongly that even while we're listening to these alluring lies we can brand them as lies and know that they are wrong. Even when we feel the flesh within us rise up and urge us to get involved with it and participate in it and not be different, we can say by the Spirit of God, "No, I've given my life to Jesus. Jesus is my authority. And he is my strength. By his grace and power I'll stand in the midst of this world." But if your Bible is closed, if you are not growing in the knowledge of the Word of God, it is only a question of time before the world will move in and take you over. You will lose all the joy and vitality of your Christian experience. That is why Jesus prays: *Sanctify them in the truth; thy word is truth.*

Jesus lived this way himself. *As thou didst send me into the world, so I have sent them into the world.* The same way. "And for their sake I have sanctified myself"—in order that they might have an example of what it means to be sanctified, to live by the truth of God in the midst of a lying world, a sick and dying world.

This is his prayer for his disciples. I hope every one of us is asking the Lord Jesus to pray for us this same way, to keep us in unity, so that nothing may break up our fellowship, our membership one with another, and to keep us from the contamination of the world around us, the lies of the evil one who would destroy us. Sanctify us by thy truth...thy Word is the truth.

Our Father, our Holy Father, we pray as Jesus prayed that you will indeed do these three things in our lives. We ask you to keep us in unity, keep us from the evil one, keep us by thy truth, and help open our minds and hearts to this truth, so that we may glorify you. We ask in Jesus' name. Amen.

12

One Body
John 17:20-26

In the greatest summit meeting ever held, the Father, the Son, and the Holy Spirit are now looking down through the intervening ages, laying out the plan and the program by which a world would be reached. The closing part of Jesus' prayer has to do with the church—from Pentecost until his coming again—including every believer who ever lived and ever will live. This is made clear in these words of Jesus:

I do not pray for these only, but also for those who believe in me through their word.
John 17:20

That gathers up the believers all over the world, who have come to Christ through the word of the apostles. Notice how our Lord indicates here the great fact which has been true throughout the ages—that there is *one* holy, catholic church. In the Apostles' Creed, recited every Sunday in many churches, is the phrase, "I believe in...the holy catholic church." Many Protestants have squirmed at that phrase, not realizing that the word *catholic* merely means universal— one universal, worldwide, holy church—not two or three, or three hundred and fifty, which is the approximate number of denominations in the United States today, but *one church*. Our Lord recognizes this in his prayer.

This is a church which stretches not only around the world but across the centuries. It has always intrigued me to remember that I am a member of the same body to which the apostles belonged, and Martin Luther, John Wesley, David Livingstone, and all the other great saints of the past; that we are as much members one of another as you and I today are members one of another in Christ. The church is one body, one great, catholic church.

And it is entered, as Jesus indicates here, only by one means—by faith in him—*those who believe in me.* It is so helpful to understand that. You do not join the church by signing a membership form, or by attending regularly, or by going through a baptism or a confirmation. These things have nothing to do with membership in the body of Christ. There is only one way: by a personal relationship with the Lord Jesus himself. In these words Jesus indicates how available he will be throughout all the course of the church age. Remember what he said at the close of Matthew's Gospel: *Go therefore and make disciples of all nations . . . and lo, I am with you always, to the close of the age* (Matthew 28:19, 20). It is this fact which makes possible that personal entrance into the church—a born-again relationship with the Lord Jesus.

Jesus of the Apostles

Notice that Jesus says this is based upon the apostolic witness—*those who believe in me through their word.* Many times I find people who attach little importance to the apostles and their writings— especially the Apostle Paul. Many people are ready to reject Paul outright. Among Women's Liberation enthusiasts he is commonly regarded as the highest expression of a "male chauvinist pig" because of some of his statements about women. Evidently these statements are not clearly understood, for no one holds women in higher regard than Paul. Nevertheless, there are many who reject the Epistles. But it must be clearly understood, and Jesus underscores it at this point, that these apostles are his chosen messengers, his chosen means of expressing himself to a waiting world. And to reject their witness is to reject him. The only Jesus we know anything about is the Jesus of the apostles.

We are being presented today with many different pictures of Jesus. There is the Jesus of *Jesus Christ*

Superstar (how I wonder who you are!), and the Jesus of *Godspell,* and various other presentations—the Jesus of the Mormons, the Jesus of the cults, the Jesus of humanism. It is no wonder that people are confused sometimes as to which is the real one. They want to ask, "Will the real Jesus please stand up?" That real Jesus is the Jesus presented by the apostolic writers. They knew him. They were chosen by him to be eyewitnesses who would convey to us the Jesus who really is. It is so important that we grasp this great fact. There is only one historic Jesus, and any deviation from the Jesus of the apostles is an imposter.

In this prayer, Jesus makes two great requests for the continuing church. One is found in verse 21: *that they may all be one*... and the other in verse 24: *Father, I desire that they also, whom thou hast given me, may be with me where I am, to behold my glory.* ... One is a prayer for unity, the other is for vision—that the church may see something. This great prayer unquestionably has been and is being answered all through the centuries of the Christian era. And we will see how it is being answered today. Let's go back now to this request for unity and see what Jesus says in connection with it:

> *I do not pray for these only, but also for those who are to believe in me through their word, that they may all be one; even as thou, Father, art in me, and I in thee, that they also may be in us, so that the world may believe that thou hast sent me. The glory which thou hast given me I have given to them, that they may be one even as we are one, I in them and thou in me, that they may become perfectly one, so that the world may know that thou hast sent me and hast loved them even as thou hast loved me.*
>
> John 17:20-23

First-Century Unity

Three times Jesus prays for the unity of the church. Note the gradual stages of growth. First he prays: *that they may all be one;* then: *that they may be one even as we are one;* and last: *that they may become perfectly one.* What is this unity? There is an effort which has been going on for some time now to bring about a union of believers, to unite them in one great worldwide church under the auspices of the World Council of Churches, or some similar organization. We are told that this will at last be the answer to this prayer of Jesus. But I find it impossible to accept that explanation. I do not believe that the church has to wait twenty centuries before the prayer of Jesus is answered, or that the World Council of Churches will accomplish what the Holy Spirit (seemingly) has been unable to do. I believe that the Holy Spirit has been answering this prayer from the very begining, and when we understand the nature of the unity for which Jesus prays we will see that the prayer is indeed being answered and has been all along.

What is the nature of that unity? Several things here in this passage give us a clue. The first is—*that they may all be one.* What does this *all* mean? If you look back you will see that he prays: *not . . . for these only.* Who are *these?* The apostles, the eleven for whom he has been praying in the previous section. He continues: *but also for those* who are to believe in him through the apostolic witness—the great body of Christians around the world and through the centuries. *These* and *those,* he now says, are all to be joined together: *that they may all be one.* In other words, the unity of the church is a unity with the apostles. We are to be made one with them. And since the primary task of the apostles was to give us the truth about Jesus, this unity is that of shared truth—one faith delivered to the saints, one record about Christ, one set of beliefs about Jesus given by the apostles. Thus, the first basis of unity in the body of Christ is the unity of shared truth. We belong to one another.

I once participated with another pastor from our church in a television panel on the subject of the church. On the panel were two local ministers from the same denomination, a rather liturgically oriented denomination. These men were disturbed by some of the things we shared about our Body Life services. (See *Body Life,* G/L Publications.) I don't think they cared much for the freedom of these services, the openness, the absence of formula, the unstructured order, for they said, "We much prefer a more ordered service. We like to go back and feel that we have a tie with the Reformation church. When we go through the Order of Service, we know that we are doing it exactly as the Christians did in the days of the Reformation. This gives us a sense of security, for it ties us in to the ancient church." I leaned forward and said, "My dear brother, I could not agree with you more. I think it is very important that we be tied to the ancient church. But why stop with the Reformation? We go clear back to the days of the apostles, and are tied in with the early Christians who spread the Gospel throughout the world in the first century." This is what Jesus is saying. We are to be tied to the apostles. The church is built upon the foundation of the apostles and the prophets, upon their witness to the historic Jesus.

Shared Power, Shared Life

Our Lord goes on to say:

> ...that they may all be one; even as thou, Father, art in me, and I in thee, that they also may be in us, so that the world may believe that thou hast sent me. The glory which thou hast given me I have given to them, that they may be one even as we are one.
>
> John 17:21, 22

Here is a different aspect of unity, based upon a glory which the Lord himself will give to the church, just as the Father had given it to him. What is this glory? Have you learned to ask yourself questions like this in your Bible study, and thus discovered the excitement of finding the clues which the Holy Spirit has given? Jesus speaks here of the glory which the Father had given him, which he gave to the church. What is that glory? You only have to look back to verse 6 to find it: *I have manifested thy name to the men whom thou gavest me out of the world;* and to verse 8: *I have*

given them the words which thou gavest me—the name
and the words of God—in other words, the power by
which the Lord Jesus has acted. He has acted always
in the Father's name, by the resources of the Father,
and according to the directions, the words, of the
Father.

Here, then, is the second level of unity—not only
shared truth, but shared power. The church is one
when it operates from the same resource and by the
same direction—by the name and the words of God.
This is the glory of the church. Have you noticed that
wherever the church begins to adopt the same means
of operating as the world around, it immediately loses
its distinctiveness and its power? As soon as we begin
to try to accomplish things by organizational tech-
niques, by mobilizing human resources, and by raising
funds—as though money were the only thing which
could accomplish what is needed—the church immediately becomes nothing more than another worldly
organization trying to make its impress upon society.

But when the church remembers that it has a unique
power which is absolutely different from anything else
—the power of the living God in its midst, the name of
God—and that it has the Word of God to direct it,
there is a glory in the church which no other organization can possibly rival. It is entirely different. This is
what Jesus prays for, that *this* kind of glory will be
visible.

Then Jesus mentions, in verse 23, the third aspect
of unity: *I in them and thou in me, that they may
become perfectly one.* That is the glory of a shared
life. Jesus in us, the Father in him, and thus, in the
remarkable words of Peter: *partakers of the divine
nature* (2 Peter 1:4). Do you believe that? Do you
ever think of yourself as linked with the life of God
—so much so that you cannot be known or understood
apart from that life? One of the reasons why we
Christians are so weak is that we will not really believe these magnificent claims about us which Scripture
sets forth. We always think they apply to someone else,
to Paul and David and Abraham maybe, but not to us.
But God insists that we are the very ones whom he is

talking about, that Jesus is in us, and God the Father is in the Son, and thus the Trinity indwells us by the Spirit, and we are linked with the life of God. The understanding of that is what produces unity among believers. Here is what Jesus is praying—that we may understand the sharing of truth, the sharing of power, and the sharing of life, and that thus the church may be one.

A Chance to Choose

What is the purpose of this unity? It is a strange kind of unity. What is it all about, and why does it exist? Twice our Lord tells us—once in verse 21: . . . *so that the world may believe that thou hast sent me* and again in verse 23: . . . *so that the world may know that thou hast sent me and hast loved them even as thou hast loved me*. First, that the world may believe that Jesus has come from God. When the church begins to demonstrate the unity of faith — of shared truth, shared power, and shared life, the world is hit by an inescapable impression that Jesus is Lord, that he indeed holds the key to history and to reality, that he is indeed the revelation of the invisible God.

Now, the world may not accept this. That is another problem. But the purpose of the witness is not to convince everybody but to give them a basis upon which they may decide. I think it is very important that we understand that the world is not necessarily going to be convinced. Many will be, thank God. Many will understand when they see that Jesus is Lord, and accept him. As Paul said, referring to himself, he was a fragrance of life unto life to some, and of death unto death to others (*see* 2 Corinthians 2:16). But in any case, God was glorified. Here our Lord reflects that same idea.

Evangelism, you see, is really intended to give everybody a chance to make an intelligent choice as to whether to accept or reject Jesus. It is to present before the world a unity so beautiful that the world will believe that Jesus is Lord. And further, that they will know that Christians are loved by God as much as Jesus is loved by God. That is an amazing testimony, isn't it? But that is what constitutes the reason for our witness before the world. As John R. Stott has so ably put it in *Our Guilty Silence: The Church, the Gospel and the World*:

Our motive must be concern for the glory of God; not the glory of the church or our own glory. Our message must be the gospel of God as given by Christ in his apostles, not the traditions of men or our own opinions. Our manpower must be the whole church of God, every member of it, not a privileged few who want to retain evangelism as their prerogative. And our dynamic must be the Spirit of God, not the power of human pesonality, organization, or eloquence. Without these priorities we shall be silent when we ought to be vocal.

So I think our Lord's emphasis on unity here is a tremendously helpful guide to our understanding of the process of evangelism and of witness before a waiting world.

Beholding the Glory

In the last section of Jesus' prayer we have a request for the vision of the church:

Father, I desire that they also, whom thou hast given me, may be with me where I am, to behold my glory which thou hast given me in thy love for me before the foundation of the world. O righteous Father, the world has not known thee, but I have known thee; and these know that thou hast sent me. I made known to them thy name, and I will make it known, that the love with which thou hast loved me may be in them, and I in them.   John 17:24-26

Jesus closes his prayer with a great, heartfelt expression of his desire that we may be with him in glory, that all who believe in his name, from the beginning of Pentecost until the end of time, may be with him in his glory. What a magnificent basis for our hope of heaven! And yet, as this makes so clear, heaven is

made heaven only because we are with Christ. This is
the hope of every believer, that one day we will be with
him. As Paul said: ... *to depart and be with Christ
... is far better* (Philippians 1:23). And in many
places Scripture brings that hope before us. The joy
of the Christian is that in heaven we behold the glory
of Jesus, the face of Jesus, the manifestation of all the
glory which is in him.

I never tire of reading about some of the troubles
and tribulations of the church in the past. One of my
favorite periods is that of the old Scottish Covenant-
ers, who stood strongly against the persecution involved
in the King of England's attempt to stamp out the
evangelical faith in Scotland. Among them was that
dear old Scottish leader, Samuel Rutherford. He was
a gracious, godly man, and a great witness to the love
of Jesus Christ. But he was placed in prison for his
testimony, and while on his deathbed he was sum-
moned by the king to appear in London to answer
charges of heresy. Samuel Rutherford sent back a
message: "Go and tell your master that I've a sum-
mons from a higher Court. And ere this message
reaches him, I'll be where few kings or great folk ever
come" (from *The Letters of Samuel Rutherford*,
Moody Press). Someone has gathered together Samuel
Rutherford's letters from prison, in which he speaks
of the joy of Jesus as he is with him there in that
prison cell. Some of his words have been put into a
song, one of my favorite hymns, which speaks of that
glory which is to come:

The sands of time are sinking, The dawn of heaven
    breaks;
The summer morn I've sighed for, The fair, sweet
    morn awakes;
Dark, dark hath been the midnight, but dayspring is
    at hand,
And glory, glory dwelleth in Emmanuel's land.

O Christ, He is the fountain, The deep sweet well of
    love!

The streams on earth I've tasted, More deep I'll drink
   above.
There is an ocean fullness His mercy doth expand,
And glory, glory dwelleth in Emmanuel's land.

ANNE R. COUSIN

It is a great hope! In the Scriptures we are not told a
lot about heaven—just enough to make us want to be
there, not enough to make us take our own life to get
there. But the hope set forth for us is that we will be
with Jesus to behold his glory in answer to this prayer.
But we don't have to wait for heaven. There is a sense
in which this prayer is being answered right now. I
think our Lord intended it this way, for in the Spirit
we are able, right now, to behold the glory of Jesus.
And it is the vision of that glory, of who Jesus is,
which changes us. Paul tells us that we are *now* seated
with Christ in the heavenly places (*see* Ephesians
2:6). And in another place he says: *And we all, with
unveiled face, beholding the glory of the Lord, are
being changed into his likeness from one degree of
glory to another; for this comes from the Lord who is
the Spirit* (2 Corinthians 3:18). So the more we see
and behold the glory of Jesus, the more we are being
made like him—even though we may not be aware the
change is taking place. Have you experienced that?
What is this glory? Our Lord defines it for us:

> *I made known to them thy name, and I will
> make it known* [I'll continue to make it known
> through the course of the history of the church],
> *that the love with which thou hast loved me may
> be in them, and I in them.*   John 17:26

The glory of Jesus is the glory of love—the love of
God for man. That is what grips our hearts and
changes our lives and makes us different people, forgives our sins, lifts us up again, and encourages our
hearts, It is the realization that God indeed loves us as
he loved Jesus.

I remember the story of the little boy who entered
a Sunday-school contest in reciting Bible verses. This
little boy happened to be a cripple—a hunchback, who
could hardly walk across the stage to recite the verses

he had memorized. As he started to hobble across the stage as best he could, with his terribly humped back, an older boy who had come in off the street thoughtlessly cried out, "Hey, crip, take the pack off your back!" The little boy broke down in tears, and couldn't go on. A man came up out of the audience and stood beside him. He said, "I don't know what kind of person would make fun of a little crippled boy, but I want to tell you who this boy is. He's my son, and he's got more courage than any of you! And I'm proud of him, because he is *mine!*" And he picked him up in his arms and walked off the stage.

I think of that story often when I read a verse like this which sets forth the love of God for us. We can understand how God could love Jesus—who wouldn't love him? But it is difficult for us to believe what Jesus says here—that we are to grasp the fact that in the manifestation of Jesus' life in us, God the Father loves us that same way. In all our hunchbacked, crippled, broken, beaten condition, he stands beside us and says, "I'm proud of him; he's mine!" And he picks us up and carries us on through life. That is the glory which Jesus says we are to behold—the glory of the love of God for us as individuals.

Not long ago, I was in Michigan at a conference, and I heard a group singing the hymn, "Near the Cross." My thoughts flashed back to a day in a park in northern Minnesota when I was just a boy, fourteen years old. I had just come to know the Lord Jesus three months before, and the glory of his presence filled my heart. I remember sitting in that park, all alone, singing that song with tears running down my face:

> Jesus, keep me near the cross,
>   There a precious fountain
> Free to all—a healing stream,
>   Flows from Calvary's mountain.
>
> In the cross, in the cross,
>   Be my glory ever;
> Till my raptured soul shall find
>   Rest beyond the river.

FANNY J. CROSBY

That is what Jesus is saying to us here. There is a
hope of glory in the future, and a present availability
of that glory to us now, so that we may manifest a
unity of love among ourselves which will cause a waiting world to know—even though they might not want
to admit it—that Jesus is Lord, and that God loves us
just as he loved his Son.